Welcome to Pallywonkersville: My Irreverent, but Humorous, Memories of Growing up in Rural Nebraska

by David Hunt

David Hunt

This book is licensed for your personal enjoyment and equipment only. If you would like to share this book with another person, please purchase it, or if it was not purchased for your use only, then please return it and purchase your own copy. Thank you, for respecting the hard work of this author.

Dedication

This book is dedicated to the women of my family who made such a difference in my life.

My Aunt Etholine, who was a college English professor when I was young. She was a strong believer in reading and education, and passed much of this on to me.

Grandmother Tilley, Etholine's sister, who also believed in reading, and in me. She and Etholine gave me presents and books to read for both Christmas and birthdays. Although I probably did not appreciate those gifts as much as I should have when I was young, they made an impact in my life and taught me to treasure reading.

Nana was my other grandmother, whom I spoke to nearly every day of my life until her death. She inspired me, and always told me I was special and would do something great one day. I am still trying.

My mother Betty, another school teacher, helped me survive many difficult times, both in health and other matters. She always believed in me.

And of course, my wife Donna is the meaning of my life. She inspires me to great heights. We have been through so much together, we have been there for each other in sickness and in health, for richer and poorer, and nearly till death did we part. If not for Donna I would not be here, and this book would not be possible. She is my reason for living, my love, and now and forever, will be my sunshine.

A very special thanks to: Belva Cassel, Bill Ainsley, and Fay Hubbard for all of their editing help. And to Valerie Veach (Pretzel) for her photo on the cover.

Contents

In the Beginning

This is a collection of short stories about the people and events that have seemed humorous to me. The names have been changed to protect the guilty. I do not know when I began noticing the funny things in life, but my cousin Chauncy Beerbaum says that he knows exactly when my warped sense of humor began.

Chauncy, who has a warped sense of humor himself, maintains that it began on a Thanksgiving Day in mid-1960. As I remember that day, it was a beautiful day for November, sunny and with a temperature probably in the upper 60s. That was pretty good for the town of Pallywonkersville out in the Midwest part of the country.

Pallywonkersville is a small town in which you can just about throw a rock from one end of Main Street to the other. Set out on the plains, it has quite a combination of small town folks, as well as farmers and ranchers who live close-by. It is the sort of town where everybody knows everybody and everybody's business. It's the kind of town that if you drink three beers at the bar, your wife will ask you why you drank three beers before you got home.

Most often this time of year was quite cold with ice and snow keeping its winter grip on everything, but this was a warm day. I lived with my mom Bertie and dad Doonie across the road from my grandma Nanna and grandpa Gaga about 4 miles out of town. On this particular Thanksgiving we had company, neighbors Ben and Emma McCarthy, and their nephew Chauncy. My grandfather's sister Eenie, who always wore a frown, was there as well.

We all had a marvelous dinner prepared by my mom and grandma, and after dessert and coffee everybody sat around for a spell to visit. I remember something about a football game, which interested the men for a while. It was the annual Nebraska-Oklahoma tussle. By mid-afternoon it was time for everybody to get up and stretch their legs; mostly I think to make room for more pie. We all decided to go outside, with the women taking a tour of the garden and hen house, while the men, me included, went for a long walk around the pig barn. We looked at the pigs, commented on what a fine-looking bunch of pigs they truly were, and generally just enjoyed the beautiful day.

After we came around the pig barn, we were in a narrow space between the pig barn and our long, four-car-length garage. It was while we were in this space that my dad decided that he needed to take a leak. This was when my new-found sense of humor came into play. Dad came up to the end of the garage and looked around the corner. There, all of the women were looking at where the garden would be next year.

Instead of moving back a ways, Dad stopped at the end of the garage and took one step backwards. Then he put matters into his own hands, so to speak, and began to pee. That is when I looked at my cousin Chauncy and he gave me a grin and a look that signaled, "go ahead." I stepped behind my dad and, with a loud war whoop, gave him a goose that was truly monumental.

Not only did he jump out from behind the garage with his man-handle still in hand, but he also let out a holler of surprise.

All of this noise and commotion alerted the women, of course, to look to see what in tarnation was going on. What they saw was my Dad in a state of complete embarrassment, being caught, as they say, with his pants down. My mom dropped her jaw and exclaimed, "Doonie! What on earth are you doing?" The other women stood there with shocked expressions, except for Aunt Eenie, who just wore a frown.

My dad quickly tried to make himself more decent and muttered something about what happens to rotten children who think they are funny. The other men, of course, thought this was the funniest thing they had ever witnessed, and that is probably why I am still here to tell the story. I was not very welcome at home that night, but Nanna and Gaga took pity on me; mostly I think because Gaga was a practical joker himself, and I had just done something that he was truly proud of, in a weird sort of way.

We're Off to See the Whizzer

The Fourth of July has had some interesting events in my family. Independence Day rolled around with the extreme heat of a summer day in Nebraska. My brother Yendor and sister Pretzel were getting very excited about the upcoming events of the day. Now that my two siblings were a little older and could enjoy the festivities more thoroughly, I can definitely say that time did not make my family any wiser.

Unfortunately for us this year, the Fourth landed right in the middle of wheat harvest. The hot weather was perfect for cutting the wheat. This being the case, my father decided that he could not have anything to do with fireworks this year. He said that it would be up to my mother Bertie and me to put on the Fourth of July festivities for Nanna, Yendor and Pretzel.

This, to me, seemed to be a perfectly acceptable idea. I was a budding young man, anxious to put on the show.

The kids were in wild anticipation all day to see the fireworks of the evening. They, of course, were able to play with the children's fireworks such as: Lady Fingers, Smoking Snakes, some Army Tanks and others of such nature. But the big ones…Aaaahhhhh…those were the things that weren't lit until it got dark. As I recall, we had a light supper of sandwiches and iced tea. Then Mom, Nanna, Pretzel, Yendor, and I all jumped into the family car, a 1965 Chevrolet Impala, four-door, maroon and black in color. This car had problems later on. Perhaps this was a precursor of that.

We drove up the road to the north forty, which at this time, were summer fallow and had recently been plowed and nothing could possibly catch fire there, right? We wanted it to be safe, since it had been a hot, dry summer this year. We drove into the field a ways, stopped the car and began setting up all of the fireworks for the night's display. Mother and I moved in front of the car about twenty yards, which seemed to be an incredibly long way for the little ones, but Nanna insisted that those fireworks be kept away from the car so nothing could possibly happen.

After winning the hundred-yard dash in the dynamite incident, Nanna was very leery to be around any fireworks at all. Mother and I were very careful to set up all of these fireworks in a perfect display on the ground. We had bottle rockets, volcanoes, flaming fountains, huge displays of Roman candles and even some of the really harmless little fireworks such as the helicopters. These were silver discs with a fan-like blade and were approximately the size of a fifty-cent piece and were one of my favorites. These little helicopters or Whizzers, as I believe they were called, went up into the air shooting off fiery sparks, going here and there, and then eventually exploding. These Whizzers were fun and harmless little explosive devices. Nothing that anyone would worry about. Right???

It was now getting about dusk, just dark enough so that we could light off many of the fireworks, much to the delight of the children. Even though the temperature outside was still about one hundred degrees, Nanna insisted that the windows of the car had to be rolled up until there was only a two-inch gap from the top, so nothing could come in. Did they have the air conditioner on in the car? Are you kidding? There was no air conditioner in this Chevy, so it was hot in there. But it was going to get hotter.

Mom and I took turns lighting the big fireworks. We were all having a very enjoyable evening, even though Nanna and the children were sweating profusely in the car. Nanna had decided that she and the kids would sit in the back seat just so they would be sure they were safe. Then to my great surprise, on the ground, I noticed that there was still a silver Whizzer left.

So for the grand finale, to end the fireworks show, I lit the fuse on the Whizzer. That was the biggest mistake I could have made. I should have just left this harmless little device alone, but gosh, what would it hurt? When I lit it and stood back to watch, the Whizzer immediately took off into the air, shooting sparks and fire all the way. It rose to a height of about four-and-a-half feet, and then suddenly changed direction and made a beeline right towards the car.

I remember thinking to myself that there would absolutely be no way that whizzer could go into the car, could it? But it did. Somehow it found that two-inch gap in the window, zoomed right over the heads of Nanna, Yendor, and Pretzel, then landed on the back deck of the seat. There it raged and whizzed, shooting out sparks everywhere, a huge orange ball of fire.

Then it came…the big explosion. I could see in the dark, the open mouths of Nanna and the kids as they were screaming at the top of their lungs and trying to get out of the car as fast as they could. Nanna finally was able to kick open one of the doors, throwing the children out into the dirt as they were screaming and yelling. As I listened, I wasn't sure if

Nanna was saying obscenities or not. Besides, my grandmother was a church going woman and surely wouldn't be saying anything like I thought that I might have heard.

Once Mom and I realized that everyone was all right, and I had a chance to stop laughing, we noticed that the car was now on fire! That orange glow in the car was not diminishing, in fact, it was getting larger. Dad's prized possession, his 1965 Chevy Impala with the black carpet was now going to be a little blacker. The carpet in the back was raging with fire. We had no fire extinguisher, so the best mother and I could do was to throw dirt by the handfuls into the back of the car, as fast and as furious as we could, Mom on one side and me on the other.

When the fire was put out, we were completely exhausted and looked like pigs that had rolled around in a pigpen. I don't think I need to embellish the look of surprise and anger that was on my dad's face, when we rolled up to the house and he saw his prized possession with the inside covered with dirt, smoked windows, and a burned back seat.

He was swearing, as he jumped up and down, even though there were small children around, exclaiming that he would never again let us light the Fourth of July fireworks, because no one else could do them right but him. At least, this was according to his outbursts and tirades. And in the end, it seemed to be all my fault. I don't know if it was so much that I was the one to light the fuse or if it was the fact that I was involved in a dynamite incident with cousin Chauncy two years before.

The Honeymoaners

They should have known. Yendor and his new bride Lena should have known it was a bad omen when Lena threw her bridal bouquet in the air at their wedding reception held at the swanky Moose Lodge, and the forty-dollar bouquet was obliterated by the ceiling fan. They should have just gone home and hidden under the bed for a couple of days. Instead my brother Yendor and Lena went on with their exciting honeymoon plans.

Their plan was to leave their multitude of children, six in total, with family, as they borrowed our sister Pretzel's Dodge Diplomat for an evening of camping, followed by an even more exciting trip to Fun World, an amusement park about two hundred miles away. Since the wedding was in July, and the weather was quite hot, a camping trip seemed to be pretty normal. Yendor and Lena loaded up the car with the tent and camping gear, filled up the cooler with beer, and headed to the area's favorite lake, Sandpit number thirteen.

When they arrived there, it was the most crowded that he and Lena had ever seen. There was no place to park, let alone set up a tent. They drove around and around for some time before Yendor saw it. He spotted a small bare spot at the top of a hill and claimed it as *Yendor's Knob*. This is not to be confused with what Lena found in the sleeping bag later that evening. It was hot, sweltering hot, so the newlyweds set up the tent, got out the lawn chairs and began to drink beer. They sat there drinking for quite some time before turning in for the night, fully expecting good weather the next day for the trip to Fun World. Yendor had not looked at the weather map which clearly showed that a massive cold front was bearing down on them, and the weather would change drastically in the night.

Lena awoke to the sound of sixty mile-per-hour wind, heavy rain and sharp lightning and thunder. "Wake up, Yendor. I think something is going on outside!"

Yendor opened his eyes, groaned, and sat up. "What in the hell is that god-awful noise, Lena?" he asked.

"Just look outside," she answered. Yendor opened up the tent flap to see a completely abandoned and barren camping area. Only Yendor and Lena atop *Yendor's Knob* were left at Sandpit number thirteen. The campground was now under attack by the elements. The wind was howling and blowing trash around like confetti. There were rivers of rainwater all around the knob. Yendor and Lena had to tear down the tent in the downpour, throw it in the back of the Diplomat and head for dry ground.

"Just our luck," muttered Yendor, "the only rain all summer and it had to happen right now. Oh well, it can't be this cold and miserable at Fun World, can it?" Just like my Dad has never learned cause and effect, my brother Yendor has never learned not to ask silly questions like this.

As they drove toward Fun World, Lena noticed they were both getting very, very sleepy. They seemed much sleepier than a few beers the night before could account for.

"My god, Lena," Yendor suddenly realized, "the car is leaking gas fumes inside, and we will have to go with the windows open the rest of the way!"

"Drive with the windows open?" she asked. "Are you out of your mind? With this rain and cold we will freeze to death in here!"

"Can't help it," Yendor said, "we have to keep the windows open or we'll die of carbon monoxide poisoning." With the windows open the two hundred miles were miserable with the wind constantly blowing the rain in the car. The heater could not keep up. Both of them were wearing shorts and tank tops. After all, it was supposed to be summer.

"We will have to stop and get some jeans and jackets," a shivering Yendor said. They pulled up to a Walmart and spent some of their honeymoon money on clothing made in China, hoping there was not too much lead in them.

Some years later, Yendor and Lena took the entire family, mother-in-law included, on a family vacation, once more in the middle of summer. Yendor again asked, "We couldn't ever run into cold weather like that in the middle of summer, could we, Lena?" You guessed it. They had to buy winter clothing for the entire family half-way through the trip. After getting some warm clothing, they continued to the Fun World without much incident, except that it was hard to listen to the radio, which only received AM stations. The only thing they could pick up was a raging, screaming Baptist preacher telling them they were going straight to hell as they drove all the way to Fun World.

"As cold as I am, Lena, hell is starting to sound pretty good!" exclaimed Yendor during the long drive. Finally they arrived, fumes and all.

"We made it!" Yendor exclaimed. With a new sense of adventure they paid forty dollars and entered Fun World to enjoy the rides. Only a handful of folks were there. Most people decided it was too cold, with the temperature about forty-five degrees and a wind of about the same speed. There was, however, one large girl from Arkansas who seemed to follow them all over the park.

"She's kind of weird, don't you think, Lena?" Yendor asked.

"Oh, she is alright, just leave her alone," said Lena. The couple decided to go down the huge water slide, the kind that goes way down, then dips back up before going down again. The top of the slide is about seven stories in the air and is wet and fast. At the bottom there is a pool about four feet deep, just deep enough to break your fall at the end. Lena went first.

"Wheeeeee!" she exclaimed as she giggled and flew down the slide. She arrived in the pool, stood up and smiled. "It was fun," she exclaimed even though she was turning blue from the cold.

"Your turn!" she hollered up at Yendor.

"Yahoooooo!" shouted Yendor as he gave a mighty push at the top and off he went. Now Yendor was about six foot, seven inches tall, and he weighed about one hundred and sixty pounds. Yes, he is just a stick. As he went down the slide a little too fast, the wind caught him when he hit the bow in the middle and sent him airborne.

"Oh, no," he thought as he found himself in the air, still going downhill. He flew over the slide and finally landed on his back at the bottom and then went head first …into the wading pool.

With his back now on fire with agony and his mind half dazed he tried to stand up and found he could not. His legs were wobbly and his back hurt. As he tried again to stand up, he saw out of the corner of his eye the big girl from Arkansas bearing down on him with a broad toothless grin.

She was going to hit him. "Oh, god, no, don't let me die here!" he thought. He tried again, more frantically now, to stand up and get out of the pool. The lifeguards finally helped pull him out just in the nick of time, before Shamoona hit the pool and sent almost all of the water out in a huge tidal wave that knocked Yendor and the lifeguards over.

"Are you okay?" asked Lena.

"Oh, dear god," he muttered. "Let's go home. I think my back is broken, and I'm freezing and having cramps." With that, they hobbled out of Fun World, returned to the gassy Diplomat, and headed home.

I don't think a word was spoken the whole way back; both were in a dark mood. But as you would guess, the sun came out when they arrived home, and it was a gorgeous day indeed. If you want to hear a litany of curse words, just ask Yendor about the honeymoon to Fun World. You will get an education for sure. By the way, do you know anybody that would like to buy some good, slightly used camping gear and a slightly gassy Dodge Diplomat?

What's Up, Dad?

My father Doonie never did learn what the word "patience" meant when he was a child. When he wants something done, he wants it done now! No excuses, no reasons why it shouldn't be done, to heck with the consequences…just do it.

When I was about ten years old, in the middle of wheat harvest, on our farm near Pallywonkersville, it had begun to rain a little bit. So we decided that we should put the wheat into the garage, in our two-wheeled trailer that someone had made for us. It was made out of an old combine bin and it was shaped like the letter "V", with all of the weight going towards the back of the trailer.

This thing, whoever made it, hadn't exactly used proper physics or mechanical engineering. All of the weight went to the back, which put a great deal of stress on the tongue of the wagon and the bumper of the truck. The wagon's tongue was made from a drive shaft, which was gotten from a huge piece of old machinery and had weld spots all over it. It was quite rusty, but you could tell that it had been painted a beautiful John Deere green, just perfect for a farm family.

Dad backed up the wagon into our very long garage. Now, this was quite the building. You could put about six vehicles end to end inside of it. We had junk piled from one end of the garage to the other, especially along the sides. Above our heads, in the rafters, boards were put there, I believe at about the time of Custer's last stand. That's when my grandfather and all of my relations began putting obsolete old junk on those boards.

There were chicken brooder houses, buckets of bolts, nuts, nails and staples; there were old mule and horse harnesses, and other items too many to mention, just because I had no idea what some of them were. Chickens liked to sit up there and they had laid eggs a very long time ago indeed. You could hear the mice scurrying around the rafters and the different kinds of birds, building nests between the boards. To top it off, all of the things that had been there for years had about two inches of dirt on them.

Dad backed up the trailer into the garage, with the pickup still attached, shut the door, and we went into the house.

The next morning, I was up for breakfast, we got our chores done and then Dad said, "David, it's time to go to town." I agreed and proceeded to the garage. Dad opened the door and grumbled," I gotta go to town and have my coffee."

"Are you taking the trailer to town too?" I queried.

"Dang blast it, no, we need to unhook it right now so I can get going. Hurry up and help me," he snapped.

I looked at the trailer full of grain, at the way the wagon tongue was pulling up on the pickup bumper and thought to myself that it looked like a bad idea to unhook it from the bumper until after we unloaded the grain. "Dad, don't you think we should empty the trailer first..."

Before I could finish my sentence Dad yelled at me. "Dang nab it, I said we need to unhook this now!"

"But Dad," I protested, "don't you think…"

Again Dad hollered, "I guess I will have to do this myself. I can't depend on you to help me do anything!" At this point Dad put a five-gallon bucket under the wagon tongue and straddled the tongue, sat down on it, and put both of his feet on the bumper of the pickup. As he reached for the pin to pull it out, releasing the wagon from the pickup, I tried one more time.

"Dad, I don't think you should pull that pin…"

"I said shut up, David. I have to get to town right now!" With that, Dad pulled the pin and pushed the wagon tongue away from the pickup bumper. Cause and effect. This is something that you should learn as a child, because if you don't, you will have some bad effects later. This is also when I learned a lesson in the laws of physics and gravity. Ignorance of these laws will not prevent you from suffering the consequences, if you ignore them.

The moment the wagon tongue disconnected from the bumper, the enormous weight in the back made the wagon stand straight up with the tongue in the air and my dad holding on for dear life with his arms and legs wrapped around the tongue like a desperate lover on prom night. Dad let out a scream, but it was short-lived as his head hit the rafters, the mass of boards, and junk and dirt from above.

The rafters and boards of the garage were, I suppose, about eight feet in the air. Unfortunately the wagon tongue, with Dad's head right at the top was at about ten feet and his head first broke one of the rafters and then went up through the boards to all of the junk on top of them.

Suddenly it was like a tornado was loose in the garage. Boards, nuts and bolts, rotten eggs, horse harnesses, barbed wire, mice, birds and, lots of dirt flying through in every direction from both the impact, as well as gravity. Chickens were trying to fly, squawking all the way. Mice were also trying unsuccessfully to fly, having just been launched from the safety of the upper regions now being disturbed. This cascade of stuff came down for what seemed like an eternity, probably only a few seconds, but what a show. Did I mention that I tried to warn him? As if this was not enough, when the roof had finished caving in on Dad, cold-cocked as he was, he let loose of his grip on the wagon tongue.

This was another error that day, as he then swung upside down, his legs still wrapped around the tongue. His legs let loose and he fell about six feet, landing square on the top of his head on the cement floor. At this point I must confess that I was pretty worried, thinking that he had to be dead. Nobody could survive all of that, could they? I ran over to him. "Dad!" I yelled, "Are you all right?"

There was no movement from him. I rolled him over on his back and looked down at him. He was covered, head to foot with dirt and rotten egg goo. His pants were ripped, mostly in the crotch area and he looked dead. "Dad!" I yelled again. "Please wake up!"

Then he did it. He opened up his eyes. His eyes were going around in different directions, much like Elmer Fudd in the Looney Tunes cartoons after suffering a similar fate. As if this was not funny enough, he then made a goofy-sounding laugh like Scooby Doo, "Huh huh hee huh."

I busted out laughing. What a sight!

By this time, my mom had arrived to see what all of the commotion was about.

"What happened ?" she asked.

I answered for him "Dad pulled the wagon away from the pickup and he flew up into the rafters. I tried to warn him but he wouldn't listen."

Mom looked at Dad, then at me a bit skeptical. She probably thought I had talked him into it. "Doonie, are you okay?" By this time Dad was able to mutter an "Uh huh," his eyes starting to focus a little better. Mom helped Dad up to the house for some medical attention. No doctors needed to be involved, as he could still walk and talk.

As for me, I got to clean up the mess, all except for the carpentry work of fixing the roof. Has Dad

learned yet about cause and effect?
Nope.

Swinging

Boner Bently was a good friend of mine back in grade school. We did lots of things together, but Boner had one great fear that caused him a huge problem on one occasion. Boner was afraid to swing on a rope: the kind that Tarzan used to swing from on the TV show. He swung from a rope that was tied up in a tree.

Once at my house in the country, Boner had a bad experience with a rope. We were playing outside, and I had a Tarzan rope tied up in a tree and we decided to swing on the rope. I swung out over a wide space first, showing Boner how much fun it was. When it was Boner's turn, I told him to grab the rope at a large knot I had tied in it. He decided to grab the rope much lower instead. As he let out a Tarzan yell and jumped away from the tree. The die was cast.

Because he grabbed the rope too low, he swung down and pile-drove himself into the ground, still holding onto the rope. He got rope burns on his hands, to add insult to injury. Boner hit the ground with a thud and did not move. I ran over and found that he was knocked silly with dirt pushed up his nose and behind his glasses. I laughed, in spite of myself.

"Are you okay?" I asked.

Boner looked up at me and said, "I ain't ever goin' to do that again!"

So here we were, with another rope to swing on. Boner, Doogie, Blower, cousin Alabama, and me, had gone down to the park and crossed the flume. It was a large metal tube that carried the irrigation canal water over the creek to the other side where there was a large bluff overlooking the creek below.

Somewhere back in time, somebody had tied a large rope to a tree branch and it hung right over the creek. Once you had retrieved the rope, you could swing clear out over the creek and back. It was a long way down and the creek was ominous looking, so it made it all the more fun to go swinging. Doogie, Alabama, and I used the rope frequently, but Boner never had.

"Nope," he answered when asked about swinging over the creek. "The rope will break, I just know it!"

"Chicken," jeered Alabama.

"Fraidy cat," both Doogie and I said to Boner in unison.

"Oh, come on, Boner, that rope is plenty strong." I said.

"No way," answered Boner. "It will break!"

"Watch this," I called out as I grabbed the rope and swung over the creek.

"Nope." said Boner.

Doogie grabbed the rope and swung over the creek as well. "See," Doogie said, "it's perfectly safe!"

"No way." replied Boner.

Finally I told Doogie, "Get on the rope and I will swing with you!" We both got on the rope and swung over the creek. This was still not good enough for Boner. Finally Doogie, Alabama and I, all three of us, got on the rope together and swung out over the creek. "Wheeee," we all called out to Boner.

"Oh, all right," he finally said, "I guess if it holds all three of you it must be safe." Well, you would have thought so, wouldn't you? It turned out that was the wrong premise. As Boner grabbed the rope, finally confident that it would hold him, he looked back at us and yelled, "Geronimo!"

As he swung out and his weight hit the rope, it broke. I still don't know how it happened, but the rope broke. Down went Boner, head over teakettle, down over and over.

"Argh!" he screamed. All the way down the hill he went. "Argh!" he yelled again. The bank of the creek was covered with brambles, yucca plants and cactus. Boner was hitting every single one of them as he somersaulted down the hill.

Doogie, Alabama, and I just looked at each other. We had looks of amazement on our faces. Boner finally landed at the bottom, with his head face down into the muddy creek water, his clothes all torn and muddy, his glasses bent and muddy as well.

"Is he dead?" Alabama asked.

"I don't know," I answered.

After a couple of seconds Boner raised his head and coughed. He turned and looked up the hill at us, mud dripping from his face.

"Guess he is all right," said Doogie.
Boner got his bearings and glared at us.

"You rotten bastards," he hollered, apparently thinking that we had done this on purpose. "I am gonna kill you all!" he screamed. Boner grabbed a huge stick like a ball bat and headed up the bluff towards us. "You are all gonna die, you sons of pig vomit!" he screamed at us.

"Uh oh, we better get out of here, Boner's pretty pissed," I said and we took off for the flume. Boner was not normally very fast, but he was mad. We were laughing at him, so he was catching up with us.

"I think he might try to kill us," said Doogie.

"We had better hurry," I answered.

"Bastards, you dirty rotten bastards, I am gonna tear you apart with my bare hands after I beat you to death!" exclaimed Boner as he got closer to us.

Doogie, Alabama and I got to the other end of the flume and ran to our bikes. "We have to slow him down," muttered Alabama as he quickly grabbed Boner's bike and let the air out of his tires. "That should slow him down," said Alabama.

"Argh!" Boner screamed. "You pig-licking sons of dog vomit!" yelled Boner, hurling the huge stick at us. He realized that now, all muddy and with his clothes ripped, he would have to walk his bike downtown in order to air his tires.

Doogie, Alabama, and I took off on our bikes. We made our escape, just ahead of the raving Boner who we thought might be foaming at the mouth by now, as angry as he was at the three of us. We laid low from Boner for quite a while until we were sure that he had cooled off from his swinging experience.

Boner never again swung on a rope as far as I know, and nobody ever put another one over the creek again. I don't think I would swing on

it now either, even if there was one.
There is such a thing as Karma, you
know.

Like a Rock

We had lots of rocks at our farm. They were everywhere. Mostly because my dad hated mud, we had rocks all over the place. I suppose we would have had blacktop if we had the money, like the Jones's at the top of P hill. They had money, so they had blacktop. We had rocks.

Dad had gone to the sandpit many times and gotten truckloads of what is known as mud rock. Mud rocks are rocks which are a sort of dull white and vary in size from golf ball up to bigger than softball size. Some are round, some are flat, but most of them are random sizes and shapes. We had what must have been a couple of semi-loads of the dang rocks on the farm and they did seem to keep the mud down. They were sure hell to ride over with a bicycle when I was a kid.

49

These rocks were not only in our driveway, but also in the pig lots, to keep the mud down there as well. I don't think the pigs liked them too much. They were too hard to lie down on and with all of the rocks, there were not very many mud holes for them to cool off in during the hot summer months.

So, on this particular day I was bored. I was probably about thirteen years old and stuck on the farm that day for some reason. Maybe my bike was broke down, or maybe I had been in trouble with Mom or Dad and could not leave. At that time, I was a baseball player for our local team at Pallywonkersville, and I was the star pitcher for that team. Since I was out on the farm, and since my brother Yendor was only about three years old, I had nobody to play catch with. Neither Mom nor Dad would play ball with me.

Mom was probably pregnant with my sister Pretzel, and Dad simply hated all sports and would not play ball with anybody. I had devised a way to throw the baseball at the back steps of our house and then play the carom off the steps, until the day I threw a little too high. The ball glanced off the top step, hitting the back screen door and making a loud BANG, causing Mom to throw a full bowl of gravy into the air. I was commanded to never again throw at the steps.

So here I was, trying to figure out a way to throw baseballs when I got the bright idea to throw rocks into the pig lot. This seemed pretty harmless since there were no pigs in the lot at the time, just rocks and weeds. I figured I could throw rocks from the driveway by the house, simply re-locating them, as nobody was around, just me and Dino, my faithful dog, who would not play catch with me either.

I picked up a small rock and threw it into the pig lot. Pretty easy, I thought. I then began hurling rocks like I was Joe DiMaggio throwing out an opposing player at home plate from the outfield fence. I picked up another rock, just a little bigger, about golf ball size. It went straight to home plate. What a throw! I found another rock just a little smaller than tennis ball size. It was a nice rock, pretty round but also very heavy, much heavier than a tennis ball. Wow, if I can throw these rocks this far, I should really be able to fire a fastball in a baseball game. The idea that throwing a really heavy object would strengthen my arm made a great deal of sense.

Zoom! I fired the rock into the pig lot and was truly pleased at the accuracy of my throwing. I looked around and found another rock. This one was perfect. It was just a little smaller than a baseball and heavy, very heavy. It was also the most round rock I had seen. It really looked like a baseball. I admired this rock for a long time. Then I picked my spot in the pig lot, reared clear back as far as I could and fired. I watched the rock fly through the air. Then, the unthinkable happened.

Dad walked out from behind the garage adjacent to the pig lot. He was carrying two five gallon buckets of pig feed down to the pig barn. He was happy at that moment. He was even whistling a happy little tune, but he would not be whistling for long.

Oh, god, I thought, it couldn't happen, could it? There is no way that rock could hit him, could it? As I watched in horror, the rock, hurtling like a missile at its target began to come down from its height and

WHAM! The rock hit Dad, not just a glancing blow, but square in the middle of the forehead! I couldn't believe it.

Upon the impact of the Intercontinental Ballistic Missile (I.C.B.M.) stone Dad went down with a thud. His feet went up in the air and both buckets of feed went flying, spilling all of the feed on the ground. Dad was down, but was he out? Surely a severe blow to the head like that would kill most people, but not my Dad. Dad had a head like a hunk of iron. It would take more than a rock to kill him, even keep him down for long.

Dad sat up, with that dazed look like Elmer Fudd. He looked around, looking for what had coldcocked him a moment before, but he could see no evidence. Of course not, the evidence blended into the background. With a million rocks around he had no way of knowing what had hit him. Dad staggered to his feet. I quickly went into the house, knowing I needed to make myself scarce. I certainly was not going to go over and tell Dad what had just happened, if I did not want to get my ass beat, or worse.

I went into the house quietly and sat down at the television, pretending that I had been there all afternoon. Soon the back door opened, and my Dad staggered in.

"Doonie, what happened to your head?" my Mom asked him, noticing a huge purple goose egg that was in the middle of his forehead.

"I don't know!" Dad stammered, still woozy. "What do you mean, you don't know?" asked my Mom.

"Dang it, Bertie, I was carrying feed to the pigs and something came out of the sky and hit me!" Dad answered.

"Well, where did it come from?" Mom asked.

"Danged if I know." said Dad.

I came into the kitchen, trying to stifle a grin and asked, "Was it a meteorite, Dad?" I, of course, knew what it was, but I was keeping mum on that note.

"I sure as hell don't know, Davy," Dad said.

"We better warn the neighbors about meteors!" said Mom thinking we needed to be responsible and warn everybody.

"Good idea," said Dad. We told the neighbors to be aware of meteors falling from the sky. Dad never did go to the doctor; he just had a hard head and went on with it, purple goose egg and all. I still have never told Dad what hit him that day. After all, I might just get a meteor shoved right up my asteroid if I did.

St. Mary's Glacier

I lived with my friend Murphy Ottnott several times when I was in my late teens and early twenties. Murphy was a trip, looking much like an old sixties hippie. He sported waist-long blonde hair, sometimes with a headband and rose-colored tinted glasses. To say Murphy liked his alcohol would be like saying that a starving man likes his food. Murphy loved to drink. If you were around him, you pretty much had to drink too. This suited me well back in those days. We both liked to party and we both liked hot women. We usually competed for the women.

It was in the late summer, we both wanted to do something different. We decided to go camping. Could we have been sane and gone to a regular camping ground up in the mountains that were a few miles away? No. We decided to go camping at St. Mary's Glacier. Neither of us had ever been there, but the mention of the name seemed to conjure up something mystical and magical about the place. This was probably due to the booze and smoke.

Murphy and I both had motorcycles. He had a souped-up little Honda, and mine was a big Yamaha with a sissy bar and luggage rack. We decided to put our cooler, small tent, and sleeping bags on my luggage rack. Then we donned our helmets and jean jackets and headed for the mountains.

It was a pretty warm day, probably in the low nineties, when we started for the Glacier. We rode and drank for what seemed to be hours. We started to reach the high ground by the time it was getting dusk, and it was getting really, really cold. The temperature now was in the forties and dropping as we rode higher. By the way, did you notice I had said St. Mary's Glacier? Yeah, it never occurred to us that glacier meant ice, which also meant dang-fricking cold! By now it was dark, around eight o'clock, and the temp down in the twenties.

"Who decided this was a good place to go camping?" asked Murphy.

"I thought you did," I snapped back.

"Well," said Murphy, "we are going to freeze to death if we stay here."

"Yep," I returned, "Guess we better head home while we can still feel our fingers."

Murphy smiled and then said," We better find some place with some antifreeze before we go all the way back down the mountain."

This seemed good to me. A bar with heat, drinks, and maybe some food sounded great. So, away we went, back down the mountain, until we happened upon a small town bar with a sign that read, "Grizzly Bear Bar," that let us know we would find what we wanted. The heat felt good as we entered, the music was not great, but the girls made up for it, sending our temperatures up quickly. Our waitress, wearing little more than a thong and a smile brought our drinks quickly and with enthusiasm, or was it just her bouncing boobs? At any rate, we drank a lot, mostly wanting our perky waitress to come back over again and again, until it was closing time. Then, without much fanfare, they threw us out into the street.

We dusted ourselves off and went to find our bikes in the parking lot. My motorcycle had electric start and started right away. Murphy, however, had a kick start and this is where the problem started. In his drunken state, Murphy stepped on his kick starter and promptly fell over.

"Gold and fricken' hell!" he hollered as he picked the bike back up.

I smiled and made some comment about electric start. Murphy shot me a stare and flipped me off. I just laughed, and he tried again. Again he fell over.

"Do you need training wheels?" I snorted.

"Kiss my angus, Dave" he shouted. About eight more times Murphy tried his kick start and fell over. I was getting almost hysterical, both from the spectacle, as well as the more colorful language coming from Murphy with each spill.

Finally the old wreck started, but then Murphy fell over again. This time the motorcycle spun around wildly on the asphalt with Murphy in the middle, screaming more obscenities. He finally got it stopped, and one more time, started it up. This time it took off in a blaze of blue smoke.

Well, I thought, I guess I'll just see him back home. I decided I was too far gone to drive back down the mountain to Corn Blossom, so I looked for a nice spot to crawl in my sleeping bag and crash. As cold as it still was, I wrapped myself around the warm pipes of my bike and dozed off.

I awoke to sunshine and the sound of rushing water. Had that sound been there the night before? I looked over my shoulder at where the sound came from and realized that in my stupor I had gone to sleep at the edge of a cliff and that a fast moving river was about sixty feet down, a long fall, if I had rolled over in the night.

Soon, to my surprise, Murphy roared in with a big grin and a bigger bottle of ripple wine. "Where on earth did you get that?" I asked.

"Found it in the Safeway parking lot, figured it shouldn't go to waste."

I could tell Murphy was feeling no pain, which probably was a good thing after his many falls.

"Let's go home," he shouted, revved up his motorcycle and away we went, down the mountain for home. If Murphy had any luck at all, that would have been the end of the story, but of course not. As we barreled down the highway, I saw Murphy look over to his right, back to the road, then back right again, staring at something on the side.

What he saw was a girl sunbathing, topless off the side of the road. I saw her, but immediately knew Murphy was in trouble. We were coming up fast on a sharp curve, with a mountain on one side and a long drop off on the other. Murphy never made the turn. He looked up just as he was about to hit the guardrail and go over the edge, several hundred feet straight down. I figured he was a goner, but he laid his bike down, hit the guardrail and then, to my amazement, slid sideways back across the highway.

Now I was trying to miss Murphy and not go over the edge myself. He hit the mountain, then bounced back across the highway again, buried his bike under the guardrail, and finally came to a stop. I stopped and ran back to see how

Murphy was. He had not been wearing a helmet. God only knew where he left that. His riding attire was sunglasses and a tee shirt. The asphalt had taken a toll. He was road rash from head to foot. Murphy looked much like a raccoon. Where the sunglasses had been was the only area on his face without a scrape. His arms and hands were a mess, especially his right hand.

"Frickin' hell!" Murphy shouted. "My bike's ruined!"

"You don't look too good either, partner," I told him. I looked at him and decided we needed to go to the hospital.

"How you going to get me there, bro?" he asked.

"Just like this." I picked him up and put him on the back of my motorcycle.

"How you going to keep me on here, Einstein?" Murphy asked.

"Just hold on." I told him. Since I had a sissy bar on the back of my bike, every time Murphy started to pass out I just pushed back and lodged him between the seat and me. We made it down the mountain, but for some reason, probably because Murphy wanted a pain killer, "Booze", we went to our friend Floyd's house. When Floyd saw us, his jaw dropped. "What in the world happened to you?" he asked Murphy.

I answered, "Murphy fall down and go boom." Floyd gave Murphy several shots of whiskey before we poured him into Floyd's car and headed for the emergency room. We waited for several hours, mostly because we had no insurance before they finally took him back to a room.

"I'm starving," I told Floyd, and we ran over to a fast food joint for a burger.

"That must have been some sight," Floyd said of Murphy's fall.

"If only I had had a camera," I said. We ate our fast food quickly and went back to the hospital. They had stitched Murphy up as good as new. He received a shot of Valium. That was a mistake. We found Murphy in the parking lot, on all fours, growling like a dog. We laughed until we cried. Then we whistled for our dog to jump in the car to go home. To add insult to injury, of which there was quite a bit, when we went back the next day to get Murphy's motorcycle, it had been stolen.

"Probably a good thing," I told him. "You're lucky that durn bike didn't kill you."

"Aw, kiss my darn angus!" was all he said.

Maggot and Morsel

There are some things that I took part in when I was younger that I am not particularly proud of, but when I look back on these memories, they are quite entertaining.

Take the events that took place one night when my friend Teddy Starr, his brother Timmie-Timeye, his friend Merlin, and I had a very interesting night out. We had all been drinking a bit, something that happened quite often, especially in our small town of Pallywonkersville, and as a matter of fact, it hasn't changed much.

My friend Teddy and I were both very good at foosball, which is a game that is patterned after soccer. The foosball table was devised of hard rubber men attached to metal rods with handles on the ends. Each participant had one set of men for each hand, with two participants on each side. The table was about four feet long by two feet wide. The bottom of the table was green plastic made to look like grass with a goal on either end. The object of the game is to simply use your little man to put the tiny ball into the other guy's goal.

As I said earlier, Teddy and I were very good at the game. The only people better than us were Timmie-Timeye and Merlin. We not only thought we were good, we truly were. We had the gloves, *stick me for our hands, and, of course,* the attitude. It was difficult for us to find anyone in the big city of Cookie-town to take us on, so we usually ended up playing games against each other. Timmie-Timeye and Merlin were a little better than Teddy and I, but not by much. So occasionally we would beat them. This would give us a good reason to celebrate, of course, with more booze.

On this evening we had played
many games of foosball and were
getting tired of it and looking for
something else to occupy the rest of
our evening. One of us, I don't
remember who, said that there was a
high school dance at the neighboring
town of Beaver Bend, and wouldn't it
be fun to go crash it? At this point, to
his credit, Merlin decided he wanted
no part of these shenanigans and went
home. The booze was working on the
other three of us, so we decided this
could be a lot of fun.

With a flip of a coin, it was
decided that I would drive my car to
the dance. My 1964 Impala, was a
big old boat of a car and was a great
party mobile. As we drove to Beaver
Bend, all sorts of ideas came to us of
how to make this a truly memorable
evening for everyone. Thankfully, we
had disregarded most of the
outrageous ideas that were thought of,

except for one. Our last idea, a truly sordid one, was for Teddy and Timmie-Timeye to scope out good-looking girls while I would pretend to be blind. Since I had my dark sunglasses in the car the idea seemed to be a perfect one. Did I mention that alcohol was involved in this devious plan?

When we arrived at the high school, I parked my car, donned my dark glasses, and we were ready to rock-and-roll. After carefully looking around, we made sure that no one was watching us. Teddy and Timmie-Timeye guided me into the building. It was a typical Midwestern small town dance, a few chaperones, lots of high schoolers and of course, a garage band that was paid way too much and knew way too little music. The way this band sounded, they were probably more inebriated than we were. Even though their sound wasn't the best, we all agreed that they did have a really cool name which was "Mud Hole".

We created quite a stir when we walked in, since seeing a blind man was about as rare as seeing a three-headed Billy goat. One of the chaperones questioned who we were, but with quick thinking, Timmie-Timeye told them that he was a brother of one of the band members, so they let us come on in. Several curious students came around us to see the blind guy, and I could tell that I was the favorite topic of the night except for who was going out parking after the dance.

Teddy and Timmie-Timeye started scoping out chicks to dance with, but the only two that seemed interested in them were a couple of unattractive girls that Teddy and Timmie-Timeye nicknamed "Maggot and Morsel." I know that those names weren't very flattering. I feel bad about it now, so many years later, but I do believe that the booze and the fact that we were young, stupid, and out to have fun also played a big part in it.

Teddy and Timmie-Timeye brought Maggot and Morsel over to talk to me. As they approached in my direction, I started rocking back and forth, with my head moving around in an up-and-down motion. I was trying to remember how the different blind musicians acted that I had seen on a few television programs. If I was going to be blind, it had to look official. The girls felt sorry for me, of course, and asked if I would like to feel their faces and get an idea of what they looked like.

Even though I was taking full advantage of the situation, I politely declined their offer, not so much because I was a gentleman, but because I could see their faces and really did not want to examine them more closely with my fingertips. The thought of how to get an idea of what their bodies, especially the top half, felt like was quite intriguing.

The girls asked me if I would like to dance with them, and I said that I would love to, but since I could not see them, it would be better to dance slow songs so that I could tell where they were. It also gave me a chance to get a bit frisky, all the while using the excuse of "Excuse me, I didn't mean to touch you there." Teddy and Timmie obliged me by getting the band to play some more slow songs, even though they were getting a bit jealous of me gaining all of the attention.

Dancing with the girls was something else. Maggot was much like the Michelin man: pretty plump and bouncy. If you moved the wrong way you might get bounced across the room. Morsel was the opposite, a very skinny girl with hips and elbows so sharp I was afraid I might get injured on her sharpness. I was able to cop a few feels without getting slapped, since I could not see what I was doing, of course.

What sorry excuses we were that night. It seemed to be an incredibly long evening. The band finally played their last song, a horrible rendition of Freebird. Then it was over. This was the part of the dance that we had been waiting for the whole evening, the grand exit. Teddy and Timmie-Timeye bid their farewells to Maggot and Morsel, as did I. The boys then led me out to the car and as they did, a large crowd of students gathered outside to watch. They looked at us with their mouths agape, as Teddy led me around the car to the driver's side. He opened my door and I climbed in behind the steering wheel. Teddy and Timmie-

Timeye jumped in the other side, I started the car, put it into gear and buried the gas pedal to the floor. I spun gravel, burned rubber and high-tailed it out of there.

The crowd went from stares of amazement to looks of anger over being made fools of. Many of them ran for their pickup trucks to chase after us and teach us long-hairs a lesson. I was a bit concerned, since the boys of Beaver Bend were long on brawn, but short on brains, and most of them sported a gun rack in their trucks. They probably felt the need to beat the dog snot out of us if they did catch us.

Thankfully I had a full tank of gas, my old Impala ran like a striped ass ape, and I knew all of the back roads like the back of my hand. You might say I could find my way home with my eyes closed, like a blind guy, riding off into the sunset.

I often think of the irony of that night, as I make my way as a blind man now. Is this a Karmic lesson? Who knows? I only know that this was an interesting night out. To this day whenever I see Teddy, we have a good laugh about that night, and then we have another beer.

Snake

Snakes. They come in all sizes, shapes, and colors. There are little snakes, large snakes, red, blue, white, black, and green snakes. Some are poisonous. Some are not. Honestly, snakes don't bother me much, not even the poisonous ones we had back in Pallywonkersville, such as rattlesnakes.

Cousin Chauncey liked rattle-snakes the best and always had some on hand, in barrels and picnic baskets mostly just to scare folks half to death, I think. I pretty much figured that I would leave the snakes alone and they wouldn't bother me either. My dad Doonie is scared to death of snakes, any kind or size makes him scream, jump, and turn white. There is only one snake that I dislike: no, I hate, really, really hate. This snake is big, ugly and menacing. It is silver and gray, and when fully extended is one hundred yards long. Huh? A snake one hundred yards long? Yep. This snake is not the living, breathing kind, but the kind of snake you clean a sewer out with.

Bobby Jones owned this particular snake and would loan it out to just about anybody, for a small fee. Bobby had one of the mechanic shops in town and always liked my little brother Yendor and me.

"Hi, Davy, hi, Yendor. How are you doing today?" he would always say when he saw us. He knew that we would take care of his snake, and we could have it whenever we wanted.

I was working for a plumber at the time and knew my stuff, or so I thought. That is probably why I received a call one evening from the local cattle ranch, the one on top of P. Hill that needed their sewer cleaned out. Pretty simple, right? I asked what the problem was, and Paul, the owner's son, told me they had a veterinarian building on the ranch that had a sewer back up and needed cleaning out. I told him what I needed per hour for the job, and we both agreed on my price.

I'd been to the ranch before and knew the building in question. It was a concrete building in which Paul used to dip cattle for lice and other vermin, castrate the males, cut off the horns from all the other calves, vaccinate them, and then send them out the other end, rather dazed and confused.

Paul and his dad used illegal Mexican labor for their ranch. Back then, we did not know what illegal aliens were, but Paul and his dad sure did. They would go to Mexico with their truck and bring a load of the illegals back to work for them. I felt sorry for these workers when I went out there, because Paul and his dad did not treat them very well. Paul knew how to speak Spanish, so I never quite knew what he was saying to them. But it sure seemed like he usually was cursing at them. He also hurled large rocks at the workers, if he did not think they were doing the job right or if they were a little too slow.

I remember one time while working on the plumbing in one of the workers' trailer house, just how illegal they probably were. In the chicken house, attached to the trailer, was a secret tunnel. If you raised the chicken roost, the whole floor came up, and there was a large room under the chicken house where the workers hid from the border patrol. Paul said the stupid workers had somehow plugged up the drain, and that it would probably not take much to fix it.

Cool, I thought, a quick job to earn a little pocket money. I called my little brother Yendor to come help me. He was excited, too, for a chance to earn a little money. As a fourteen-year-old he had things to buy. I told Yendor it would probably take just a half a day. We would start Saturday morning and have the rest of the weekend to play. I told my wife at the time, Low-rider, that I would be busy Saturday, and went to Bobby's shop and got that snake.

I put the snake and some tools in my old Chevy pickup and went to my parents' house to get Yendor. Out to the ranch we went, not knowing the nightmare we were walking into.

When we got to the ranch, Yendor asked, "How long do you think this will take?"

"Probably get done late this morning." I answered. We arrived and went to the vet building. Paul let us inside, showed us where the drain was, and told us he would check on us later. I said, "Should get done this morning." Paul left and we got started. I began running the snake down the drain, a large six-inch pipe, and soon realized we were in trouble. I brought up from the drain several five-gallon buckets full of cattle horns, rubber ear tags, and, of course, cow poop.

"Oh, good lord," I told Yendor, "this really sucks. I hope we get to the blockage pretty soon."

"Me, too," said Yendor, "I would like to go swimming this afternoon." If he meant that he would like to go swimming in cow poop and cattle horns, he would get his wish. We worked for about an hour and had gone only about fifty feet. We were bringing up buckets and buckets of horns, tags, and liquefied manure.

"How much longer, Dave?" asked Yendor.

"I sure hope pretty soon." I replied grimly. From time to time, we would catch a glimpse of the Mexican workers looking at us and laughing. They knew what was down the drain, because they had put it there. My feelings of sadness about how these workers were treated was starting to turn into a deep dislike for them. I was thinking I would like to stuff them down this drain myself.

At noon we had gone about two hundred feet and pulled out enough to fill up a pickup truck, still no closer to the blockage. Yendor and I, both filthy and wet, drove to town for lunch. Because we were in such a sorry state, we went to my house for lunch, instead of the café.

When we walked in, Low-rider asked, "How's it going, guys?" One look at the two of us and she soon knew it had been a silly question. We were not in the mood to talk much. She made us eat our sandwiches outside on the porch, and we were quickly back to the hell hole.

Surely, Yendor and I thought, the blockage had to be found soon. It could not be that far down the drain, could it? The drain tube was nearly a quarter of a mile long, over two hundred yards, and then it emptied out into a canyon. I wonder if the E. P. A. knows about this? We ran the snake again, bringing up more and more of the foul stuff. At about four o'clock, two more trucks of stuff later, we were at the end of our snake coil, and still had not found the plug.

"What are we going to do now, Dave?" Yendor asked.

"We are going to have to find out where the pipe goes through, dig down to it and break a hole open so we can go further down with the snake."

"Oh, god!" exclaimed Yendor. "Can it get any worse?"

Again, we should never ask these kinds of questions, because the answer will always be yes! We dug for almost an hour and no pipe. Finally Yendor said "Maybe I can use a couple of pieces of brass wire and find the pipe by dowsing."

"Give it a try," I said, "we have no better ideas."

Yendor took a couple of brass wires, bent them like the letter L and began walking back and forth at about the point we thought the pipe should be. Soon the wires crossed each other quite a ways from where the pipe should be and he announced, "Bingo! Here it is!"

I had my doubts, but what the hell, we gave it a try. What do you know; there it was, down about eight feet. We dug a fairly large hole around the pipe and then Yendor asked, "Now what do we do?'

"We knock a hole in the pipe, if we are lucky, it will be dry inside."

"What if it ain't?"

"Well," I answered, "then we are unlucky, and we will have a massive fountain of crap to deal with." Yendor jumped out of the hole at this news. I grabbed an axe and swung it and hit the pipe square in the middle. We were, very, very unlucky. The pipe erupted in a huge gushing fountain of, you guessed it, cattle horns, ear tags, and liquefied cow crap. "Gold and rotten sons of dog biscuits!" I hollered.

Yendor was amused by my ravings but one glance from me quieted him down.

"We will have to see how much is in there." I said as we got the buckets and the foul stuff out of the hole. Many buckets and many new curse words later, we had the hole empty. I climbed in with the snake to start down the second end of the pipe. At this point, if the illegal workers had stopped by they would have been permanently entombed in a hole of cow manure and cattle tags.

After about two more hours, with sunset bearing down on us, we hit it. But now the snake could not go through something we hit, nor could I pull the snake back out. "Oh, good lord," I muttered. "We will have to dig down where we think the blockage is and pull it out from there!" Yendor found the pipe again with his dowsing and we dug down. Somewhere near China, we again made a hole. This time we were lucky.

"Hooray!" exclaimed Yendor, as we found the blockage in the pipe. As we pulled it out, it began to dawn on us what had happened.

"It's a dad-burned horse blanket!" I exploded.

"What would a blanket be doing down there?" asked Yendor.

"There is only one way," I began. "It had to be put there on purpose by some lazy good-for-nothings that wanted to get out of work!"

By this time, Paul and his dad, not too happy with how long we were taking, came over to the hole, and I showed them what had caused the problem. Paul immediately went to the illegals' trailer and there were horrible sounds indeed emanating from inside, with much Spanish being hollered, and I wished I knew what was being said. Yendor and I patched the holes in the pipe, filled the holes in the ground, and got our check, a sizeable one for us, but really not worth it in the long run. We drug our tired asses home.

A few weeks ago, Yendor called me up and said that he had run into an old friend of mine. When I asked who it was, he answered, "Not a person, Dave, but a thing-- ugly silver and gray thing."

"What are you talking about?" I asked.

"Well," said Yendor, "payback is a bitch, big brother. I found that old snake we used at the feedlot years ago at an auction. I bought it for twenty dollars, and I intend to drum up some business for us to use that stinking thing again!"

If my wife Melanie tells me that Yendor is at the door with a smile on his face and something big and ugly in his truck I am going into hiding in the witness protection program.

Goin' Ape

My father Doonie is jumpy. That is a complete understatement. Doonie will jump six feet in the air if you just yell "snake." If there really is a snake, get the hell out of the way, or you might get run over in his stampeding haste to get away.

Because of this rather humorous sense about Doonie, there have been quite a few practical jokes played on him over the years. It seems that almost everybody in Pallywonkersville either wanted to get in on one of these pranks, or at least be there to witness the fun.

Such was the case one hot summer day, when I was a young boy. I was playing in the yard when I heard the familiar rumble of our tractor, coming down the lane to our house with what I believed to be some kind of siren blaring. When I turned to look, I saw that our tractor was moving at top speed toward the yard, and the siren I thought I heard was my father calling Mom's name at the top of his lungs. "Bertie!"

When Dad yells Mom's name, it is always at the top of his lungs. At the dinner table, he sounds like Fred Flintstone yelling "Wilma!"

"Bertie," he screamed with a completely wild-eyed look about him. Whatever was going on, Dad had just had the crap scared out of him, and I do mean that literally. Mom came out of the house to see what on earth was happening, just as Dad rounded the corner of the house, slammed on the brakes of the tractor, and brought it to an abrupt halt.

"What on earth is going on, Doonie?" Mom asked.

Dad's answer caused both Mom and me to look at him and say, "Huh?"

Dad screamed at us, "Get the guns, Bertie, there's a gorilla in the corn field. I just barely got away. We have got to go back and get it!"

Growing up in Pallywonkersville, we had seen quite a few things: wild animals, and more than our share of strange people. A gorilla seemed pretty unlikely, but Dad was insistent.

"Are you sure it was a gorilla, Doonie?" Mom asked him.

Dad bellowed at her, "It's a gol-durn gorilla, Bertie. I know a gorilla when I see one!" Living in Nebraska all of his life, how would Dad really know a gorilla? He did not like to go traveling, so I was sure that he had not seen a gorilla in the zoo, since we had never been to one. But the story he told was getting interesting. Maybe a traveling circus was going through town, and a gorilla had escaped. I hoped, if that were the case, I could see some tigers, lions, and monkeys.

"Damn it, Bertie, we got to get that gorilla!" Dad was getting antsy. He and Mom went inside the house and got the guns: a 22 caliber single shot rifle and a 410 single shot shotgun. These guns were more likely to piss a real gorilla off than to kill it. They left me at the house and went roaring after the gorilla toward the corn field in the north forty.

I contemplated what I would do if the gorilla and all the other killer animals suddenly showed up at our house with Mom, Dad and the guns all gone up north. I could just take a chair and a whip and tame them. Wouldn't that be cool? I went inside, looking for a chair I could hold up. I made a whip out of a broomstick and a piece of rope, just in case.

Pretty soon, much to my disappointment, Mom and Dad came home. Dad was still white as a sheet and shaking. Mom continued to ask, "Doonie, are you sure it was a gorilla?"

"I know what it was, Bertie, it was a gol-durn gorilla!" Dad exclaimed, "Do you think I am crazy? It was a dang-gone gorilla!" Whether or not Dad was touched in the head could sometimes be debated. He sure seemed certain on this one. Dad sat down and opened a beer.

"Bertie," he said after he took a few gulps to settle his nerves, "I was making a round with the one-way," (a farm implement much like a disc.) "I was just a few rounds in, about fifty feet from McClonsky's corn field, and I looked over at the corn. All of a sudden I saw something in the corn, kinda down on the ground, and I thought to myself that it looked like a little bear. I said to myself, what a cute little bear. I wonder how it got in the corn field.

"Then it stood up and began pulling corn out of the ground, beating its chest and throwing corn stocks up in the air and looking right at me, like I made it mad and it wanted revenge!"

"It was a little bear doin' all that, Doonie?" Mom asked.

"Hell, no, it wasn't a bear," hollered Dad. "It was a gol-durn gorilla, about ten feet tall, just beatin' his chest and coming after me fast as lightning!"

"Oh, my gosh," Mom said, still trying to figure out if Dad saw a bear or gorilla. Neither is indigenous to Nebraska.

"Are you sure it was a real gorilla?" I asked.

"I know what I saw, gol-dang it!" Dad bellowed.

Mom went to the other room and brought back a book and gave it to Dad.

"What the heck is this for?" yelled Dad.

"Well," Mom said, "look in the animal book and see if you see the same thing in there."

"Oh, all right, I still know what I saw, and it was a gorilla!" Dad exploded. In just a few seconds, Dad said, "Ah ha, there it is, it's not just a gorilla. It's a frickin' gorilla, it is!"

"Doonie," Mom exclaimed, "watch your language around David!"

I was astounded that Dad just said frickin' since it was not one of the tame words he usually used around me.

"So, it was a frickin' gorilla" I asked?

Whap, I felt the sting of my Mom's hand as she whacked me and said, "We don't use that kind of language, young man!"

"But Dad said it" I stammered, acting hurt, although I actually thought this was absolutely hysterical.

"Bertie, it says it right here." Dad pointed to the book. I looked and saw the picture of a gorilla with the caption underneath (African Gorilla).

"Yep," I said, "it looks like it says a frickin' gorilla all right!" Mom just glared at me, knowing that it was simply Dad's mispronunciation. But you could never talk him out of the truth about what kind of gorilla it was now. It was forever, a frickin' gorilla.

Now, of course, came the realization that, whether it was an African gorilla or a frickin' gorilla, what Dad said he saw in the cornfield was indeed a gorilla. Dad took a few more drinks of beer and got back to his story. "I saw that frickin' gorilla coming after me, and I knew that I had to give her hell and get out of there! I reached back and pulled the pin out of the one-way, put the tractor in high gear and gave it the gas!" Dad recalled. "All of a sudden I felt that awful ugly thing grabbing my behind, and then it slapped me in the rump. I thought I was a goner for sure but I got away, just barely."

The truth, as we later found out, was that Dad had a rope attached from the tractor seat to the one-way. When he pulled the pin, it left the one-way in the ground, and the tractor took off without it. The rope pulled the tractor seat down, almost to the ground, before breaking and sending the seat back with a huge kerthump, hitting my Dad in the rear end, making him think that he was about to be grabbed.

"It was terrible, just terrible," Dad said, still shaking but starting to calm down a bit. Suddenly he jumped up and exclaimed, "We've got to go and warn the neighbors. I got away from that thing but they might not be as lucky!" We jumped into the car and roared off to our neighbors, the McClonskys, who lived just a mile south of us. We came screaming into the yard and stopped in a cloud of dust. Dad yelled for Bub McClonsky to come out of the house, there was an emergency to be talked about.

Bub walked out and said "Doonie, come on in the house, you too, Bertie and David." I noticed that Bub was trying to keep a grin off of his face. I wondered why he was grinning at a time like this. It was an emergency. We went into the house and sat down at the kitchen table with Bub and his wife Edna.

Bub was still trying to stifle a grin as he asked Dad, "What is going on, Doonie?"

Dad began, "You are not gonna believe this. There is a frickin' gorilla in your cornfield up north, Bub. We need to kill that ugly thing. Bertie and I went up there with the guns, but could not find it. We need you to help us, before it gets somebody!"

At this statement, Bub lost his grin. He turned white and said, "Oh, god, Doonie, I think we need to tell you something before somebody gets hurt."

"What the heck do you mean, Bub," Dad asked.

"Well," said Bub, "I think Melvin and Chauncey need to tell you something. Come on down, boys," hollered Bub. Soon Bub's son Melvin and his cousin Chauncey came down the stairs with sheepish grins on both their faces.

"You want to tell Doonie what is going on, boys?"

"Well, Doonie, we owe you an apology," said Melvin.

"What do you mean?" asked Dad with a bit of a confused look on his face.

"Well, said Melvin, "that was no gorilla you saw in the corn field, Doonie."

"The hell it wasn't!" Dad yelled. "I know what I saw!"

"Calm down, Doonie." Chauncey said. "It wasn't a gorilla you saw. It was Melvin and me."

Now Mom and Dad were looking at each other, Melvin, Chauncey, and Bub with looks of total confusion. I was confused myself. I might be able to see how Dad might confuse a bear and a gorilla, but how could he confuse Melvin or Chauncey for a gorilla?

"Go ahead, boys, and explain," Bub said.

"Well," Melvin started, "we were just playin' a little joke on you, Doonie. You see we got this gorilla mask and an old raccoon coat, and we thought we could scare you a little. We didn't want anybody getting hurt." With that Melvin brought out a gorilla mask and Chauncey produced an old raccoon coat, the kind college kids wore in the twenties.

"You see, Doonie," Chauncey said. "I put on the coat, Melvin put on the mask and sat on my shoulders, and we made like a screaming mad gorilla just to see if we could scare you."

By now both Mom and Dad were getting a little hot. Dad said, "You could have got yourselves killed, you numbskulls. Why I could have shot you!"

"Well," said Bub, "I think that the boys owe you an apology, but no harm was done, Doonie. I think the boys can even do your field work for a while, right, boys?"

107

"Right" both boys said in unison.

So the frickin' gorilla was no gorilla but a frickin' good joke, one that none of us will ever forget. I wonder if I put on the mask and snuck in Dad's living room..no, better not, he still has those guns, you know.

Skunked!

Ronnie Bird was a good friend of mine, and he told me that his grandparents were hillbillies who, for many years, lived in the backwoods of the mountains in a small cabin. Ronnie said that going to Grandma and Grandpa's house was an adventure indeed, complete with shooting lessons, tobacco chewing games, and, of course, dinner with possum pie, grits, and turnip casserole.

Living back in the hills did have its drawbacks though, such as having no running water or electricity. Yep, the old outhouse was the only way to go, if you know what I mean, and the only heat source was an old fashioned pot-bellied wood burning stove right in the middle of the living room. This presented an incredible problem one cold winter night as Ronnie's Granddad, Claude, had to go pretty bad, even though it was cold and dark outside, but dagnabit he had to go! So out he went, wandering in the dark to the cold outhouse. But that wasn't the problem. The incident occurred when Claude tried to come back into the house.

Claude thought he smelled skunk when he went to the outhouse, or was it just the deposit he unloaded after eating Nellie's squirrel stew. Nope, as Claude would soon find out, it was a skunk. As he opened up the front door to come in, the skunk, probably half-starved and rabid, made a mad dash into the house just ahead of Claude.

"Jumpin' Jehosephat!" hollered Claude as he saw the skunk race into the house.

"What in tarnation?" yelled Grandma Nellie, and then she saw the skunk. "Oh my Lord, Claude, get that thing out of here!" Nellie hollered as the skunk began to run around the living room. To this point Claude and Nellie had been lucky. Though the skunk was in the house he had not sprayed his foul perfume yet.

"Get him out of here right now!" bellowed Nellie.

"How in tarnation am I gonna' do that, Nellie?"

"Chase him out of here, Claude," said Nellie.

It was then that Claude had a bright idea, but it was one that he would regret. "I got it!" he shouted, and then he grabbed Nellie's new broom and stuck the straw end into the potbellied stove.

"What on God's green earth are you doing with my new broom?" asked a bewildered Nellie.

"I am gonna' scare him out of here all right!" yelled Claude. The broom was now burning brightly, and Claude began to chase the rabid skunk with the newly lit torch. It was a really bad idea. The skunk, now frightened by the fire, sprayed and scored a direct hit on poor old Claude.

"E-gad!" gasped Claude, as the skunk's spray hit him in the face. Now half blinded by the spray, Claude lunged with the torch to rid the house of the foul intruder. Instead of scaring the skunk outside, however, he lit the skunk's large bushy tail on fire.

"Dear God, Claude, that thing is gonna burn the house down!" screamed Nellie. At this point, the skunk, both panicked and on fire, began to run around the living room, spraying wildly as Claude yelled and Nellie shrieked. The flaming skunk, not having done enough damage already, now raced into the kitchen.

"The house is on fire, Claude," Nellie screamed.

The flaming skunk now raced into Claude and Nellie's bedroom, all the while spraying even more of his foul skunk juice. He crawled under their bed, catching it on fire before he died of his wounds.

"Get some water," hollered Nellie.

Both she and Claude raced to the well with buckets and valiantly put out the fires in the kitchen and their bedroom, all the while coughing and gasping from the incredible noxious smell made by the flaming skunk. The couple looked around at what, just minutes before, had been their quiet, happy home, but was now a complete disaster area.

Claude and Nellie never did get all the skunk's stench out of the old house. They eventually just got used to it, but they never did have much company come for dinner, even for Nellie's famous raccoon stew.

Many years later, the elderly couple moved to town, and it was just their luck that when they got their first television set, the program that came on was a Bugs Bunny cartoon. Yep, you guessed it, Peppe lePew. Claude screamed and grabbed his shotgun this time, instead of a flaming broom, and blew the brand new TV to smithereens!

Roped

If you were to look up the word "jumpy" in the dictionary, you would most likely see a picture of my dad Doonie. Dad resembled Don Knotts, both in appearance and in how easy it was to scare him. Few things scared him more than snakes, especially rattlesnakes, of which there were quite a few out on our farm, and really could be a hazard to human health.

So, all you had to do was holler "snake" and you could get a good rise out of Dad, usually a good scream, and he probably would jump in the air and run as well. This proved to be great entertainment to all the fellows downtown. They tormented Dad with rubber snakes, whenever they wanted a good laugh, and Dad never disappointed them.

On this hot summer day when I was about ten years old, I was sitting in my tree house and feeling bored. I had my bb gun and had shot at as many imaginary villains as I could, and was looking for something else to humor me. My tree house was pretty cool. It was about twenty-five feet in the air, built where five trees had grown up from the same stump and spread out as they rose higher. Where the tree house stood, the width came to about eight feet across, so my tree house was huge. I had also made walls on the sides nearly four feet high, and I'd made a trap door with boards nailed on the inside of one tree to climb up. But once in the tree house, you could keep anybody else from getting up there by simply sitting on the trap door.

The final component to this marvelous tree house was a fireman's pole at one end, so you could jump out, slide down the pole, and make a quick getaway. Did I mention that I also had in the tree house a huge coil of old brown rope? Yeah, this old coil of rope was as big around as a man, about three feet high and as I had found out, completely worthless because it was rotten and would not support much weight.

So there I was, bored, when my dad Doonie walked under the edge of my tree house and began pulling weeds next to the fence by our chicken yard. I remained quiet and watched him right there below me. He had no idea that, above him, I was lurking, and that I was beginning to formulate a devious plot that would scare the bejesus out of him.

Yep, I looked at the rope, then at Dad, then at the rope again. I just had to do it, I simply could not resist. The spirit of my cousin, Chauncey Beerbaum the prankster, was upon me. I quietly slid the huge coil of rope to the edge of the tree house and waited for Dad to get to just the right spot. When he finally did, I gave the rope a shove over the edge and, in my loudest and deepest voice, yelled, "Snake!"

My dad, hearing the word "snake," looked up instinctively to where he had heard the voice. As he looked up, the gigantic old coil of rope, looking to him like some monstrous, huge, flying rattlesnake landed on top of him and literally went over both of his arms, pinning them to his sides.

"Arrrrghh!" my dad screamed in terror, realizing the huge snake was now coiled around him. "Arrrgh, snake, goldurn snake, arrrgh!" he hollered again at the top of his lungs. He also began writhing around on the ground trying to get away from the awful monster. I watched as he tore the old rope to pieces. All the time screaming, "Snake, snake, dadburned snake!" and flailing wildly.

It was all that I could do not to bust up laughing at the spectacle, but I knew if I did I would probably be dead meat. After several minutes of this hilarious, snake-wrestling death match, Dad began to realize that he had been had. The look on his face was priceless, but the look of bewilderment soon turned to pure anger as he figured it out.

It was then that Dad began to look up, remembering the voice from above that started the whole ordeal. Covered with dirt and sweat and red in the face with anger, he bellowed, "David, I am gonna' kill you!"

I was still laughing hysterically, but realized as Dad started up the steps to my tree house that I had better think fast. "Why, you rotten little son of a hog's ass, you are gonna' get it now," he screamed as he got closer.

I knew Dad was too big for me to sit on the trap door, so I let him get all the way to the tree house and part way through the trap door before I jumped on the fireman's pole and slid down, hitting the ground running to make my escape.

"Come back here, you rotten little turd!" he hollered as I took off. I knew that he could not catch me now, as I ran for the canyon behind our house, my usual refuge when I was in trouble. For a long time, I heard Dad yelling for me to come back, but I just laughed to myself as I mused over what a perfect prank I had pulled over my old man.

Dad eventually went to town for coffee and had calmed down a lot by the time he came home. Perhaps he had a few beers as well. I just know that he most likely did not tell the guys downtown about the monster snake which turned out to be just an old piece of rope. I also know that Mom probably kept him from tying me up with what was left of it and hanging me upside-down from my own tree house.

Mudder's Day

Mom and Dad argued a little, but not too much, probably like many other couples. Most of the time I just tried to ignore their arguments. Once I had called my grandmother up during one of their fights, and was told by all parties involved that it was none of my dang business. I was the one who got in trouble for tattling.

So I don't know if they had a spat that morning or not. I just know that it had rained for a few days, and the gravel road from our house to town was a real muddy mess. Anyway, Mom got my brother Yendor and sister Pretzel ready for school, fed them their breakfast, and then loaded them up in the car, an old, dark green, 1970 Chevrolet Impala, and away they went.

Even though it was muddy that day, Mom had on a new dress that she wanted to show off at school and could not wait for sunny weather to do it. Yendor and Pretzel didn't ride the school bus, because Mom was the Home Economics teacher at Pallywonkersvill High School, and she drove the kids to school with her every day. So today was like any other, except for the lots and lots of mud.

Mom was always a good driver, but that day it didn't help her. The mud was just too much. As the car slipped and slid down the road, she encountered a rut going down the hill to the first canyon. It led her right towards the ditch.

"Look out!" she exclaimed as they went into the ditch. Luckily Mom and the kids were going slow, so the Impala just slid into the ditch a little way, but with all the mud, Mom could not get it back on the road.

"Oh great, now I have to walk back and get Doonie to pull us out." She told Yendor and Pretzel, "You kids just stay here, and we will be back soon and get the car out."

My brother and sister were actually excited by this turn of events. First of all they would be late to school, and secondly they would have a good story to tell all of their classmates. It's not every day you are on the brink of certain death at the edge of the canyon. Mom slogged her way the mile and a half back to the house in her new dress and found Dad.

"What the devil are you doing back here, Bertie?" Dad asked.

"Oh, Doonie, the kids and I went off in the ditch, and I need you to get the truck and come and pull us out."

"Oh, for cat's sake!" bellowed Dad, "Can't you do a simple thing like drive to town?" Yep, Dad was in a bad mood and Mom was getting the brunt of it. "Get in the dang pickup!" Dad yelled at Mom.

"Oh, all right!" she snapped back. Neither of them spoke during the trip to the car. They were each miffed at each other, and the old Ford F150 pickup was loud.

They soon arrived at the car to find Yendor and Pretzel, listening to the radio at near full blast.

"You kids better not have run that battery down or you're gonna get what for!" Dad hollered.

"Oh, leave those poor kids alone, Doonie!" Mom shot back. This made Dad even a little hotter. Then he had to get under the car in the mud to attach the log chain to the car bumper.

When he had finished connecting the chain to the car and pickup, he told Mom to get in the car, start it up, and hold on to the steering wheel until he told her to let go.

"All right," Mom said, "just don't act like a durn fool any more in front of the kids!" Dad did not like taking advice from anybody on anything, not even Mom. He revved up the truck, let out the clutch and took off. Dad had Mom out of the ditch in just a few yards, but that was not good enough for him.

"Whoa, Doonie!" Mom hollered as they took off, but then Dad got even more carried away. He floored the old pickup, and it started spraying mud with the back tires, and most of it was going on the car.

"Stop, you durn fool," Mom screamed to no avail. Dad either could not hear her or simply did not care what she said. He was on a mission now to drag her all the way to town. But not before he sprayed even more mud on the poor old Impala, which now looked like some mud monster out of a horror movie. Dad kept the pickup floored, until he had the car completely buried in about 3 inches of mud from front to back, top to bottom.

"Wheeeee!" screamed the kids, "what a fun ride!" Mom did not say another word. She just held the steering wheel in a death grip, hoping not to hit anybody, since she had no control of the speed of her Chevy missile, and she could not see where she was going. She was like a blind woman, driving in the Daytona Muddy 500. Then her worst fear came true, as she swerved just the slightest, as a neighboring farmer was coming the other way and the old mud bomb side-swiped him.

127

"Gol dang it, Bertie, can't you drive better than that?" Dad hollered as he saw the side of his car, now covered in mud, but also with a large dent in the side. Dad floored the pickup even more. Then instead of stopping at the bottom of the hill at the highway, like a sane person would do, he simply made an abrupt left turn onto the highway.

"Oh Lord, help us, hang on kids!" hollered Mom as she tried to make the abrupt left turn as well. The kids swayed back and forth, thinking this was the most fun they had been part of in a long time. Of course, no seat belts were being used then. I don't know if the old Impala even had them. Dad got both vehicles up to about 90 miles per hour, and Mom and the kids hung on for dear life. Dad slowed down just enough to make the turn into Pallywonkersville. Then he drove straight to the school and stopped right in front of the school house and jumped out of the pickup.

"Well, Bertie, here we are, are you happy?"

"Happy about what, that you almost got us killed back there?" Mom screamed. "Are you crazy, Doonie. Look what you have done to our car!"

By now there was a huge crowd of students and teachers outside, looking at the damage that had been done to the old Impala. It was a mess, with so much mud you could not tell what kind of automobile it was. But you could certainly see that the driver's side was caved in. Mom and Dad fumed at each other for some time about whose fault all this was, and I don't know who cleaned up the car.

I laid low for a while myself, trying to stay out of the whole thing. Yendor and Pretzel did tell me later that they had a great time at school that day, telling everybody about the best ride they ever had.

Independence Day

My family has always enjoyed the Fourth of July. From the time that I was a little kid, I remember fireworks, firecrackers, bottle rockets, Lady Fingers, Smoking Snakes, many of which are now illegal in most states. Although many people would drive from Nebraska to towns in Missouri to get the illegal treasures.

When I was somewhere in the neighborhood of eight or nine years old, I don't remember which, we had had a marvelous Fourth of July, with my Mom and Dad setting off firecrackers. My grandparents and I were in the background, watching with awe the glorious sights and sounds that the fireworks made. It ended with the last firework, the big mamma, the big kahuna, a firecracker of truly gigantic proportions, at least to someone who was nine years old.

This firecracker was about three feet tall and as big around as a baseball bat. It had a big wooden base and a picture of Uncle Sam smiling wide on the front of it...truly a magnificent fixture. I was so excited about this big kahuna firecracker as my father lit the fuse.... Then we waited, and we waited... and we waited some more.

It finally became apparent after much anticipation, that the big kahuna was a big dud. What a bummer. All of my family's anticipation to see the biggest firework of all, and it didn't shoot off.

We had waited for all of the beautiful sprays of blues, greens, and red sparkles, and most of all I was looking forward to the many loud bangs that would come with the wonderful color display. I was truly bummed out after witnessing that disappointing event.

My father took the firework and put it into the trash barrel in the garage. The next day was a rainy one. While my Mom and Dad were out doing something, I'm not sure what…a thought occurred to me…what if Big Bertha could be salvaged. Could it be that it just might need some more fire power to get it going?

Could it be that it just had a bad fuse, and the firework itself was perfectly good? Knowing that the trash barrel was in the garage and not outside where the firecracker would get wet, I went to investigate the situation.

There she was. Big Bertha …in all her shining glory, still sitting in the trash can, but still very much intact. Thank goodness my Dad hadn't beaten it to a pulp because she hadn't gone off. He had simply put her in the trash can.

I wasn't supposed to play with matches, unless I was lighting firecrackers, but I went up to the house to get some of our long kitchen matches. It came in handy that I still had a few firecrackers and Red Rats, which were small red firecrackers that, when lit, would take off like a wild rocket with no particular direction until they exploded. So, with a punk in hand and some matches, I went to retrieve Big Bertha. Mom and Dad were nowhere to be seen, so I took Big Bertha out to the driveway, where all was clear.

I looked at the top of the firecracker, and it appeared that if I dropped a match inside it, there would be some sort of chain reaction to set things off. I was going to find out, wasn't I? Then I lit a kitchen match and dropped it into the top...stood back a safe distance and waited....and I waited...and I waited some more. Of course, much like before, my expectations turned to feelings of "here we go again". Big Bertha is still a dud.

But maybe it wasn't really a dud...maybe the match just went out before it had reached the wick. Perhaps the amount of wind force after dropping it in so far put it out. Carefully I crept up to the firecracker, and I listened. After hearing no activity coming from inside the firework, I decided that I would just peer over the edge to see if indeed the match is still going.

As I peered over the edge of Big Bertha, it was the exact time that the first of a number of huge screaming fireballs shot out of the top. I remember seeing a fireball just in time to close my eyes and try to pull my head back and whoosh...it went right over my head or at least I thought so.   Boy that was close! Then I smelled the indescribable scent of burnt hair. Sure enough, I put my hand on my head and my short hair, that I had just a few moments ago, was now gone, especially down the center. Only a trail of short blackened stubble was left. I panicked. What were Mom and Dad going to say?

I ran into the house…where there was no one to be seen. I looked into the mirror, and it was worse than I had expected it could possibly be. There I was, staring at myself. I saw a six-inch wide streak of blackened, curly, crinkly stubble running down the middle of my head where my hair used to be. If that wasn't bad enough, my eye brows were gone too! In their place were little singed remnants of what used to be black hair. I decided to scrub my head to get as much of the burnt-looking stuff out of my hair as possible. This didn't work that well.

It's kind of tough to be inconspicuous when there is hair on both sides of your head, nothing in the middle and no eyebrows to be found. It attracts a lot of attention.

What I needed was a good plan. Since hats were not allowed in the house, that idea was out. Although it would have been a good one. Perhaps I could have put this problem off for weeks.

Then it had occurred to me…the "Red Rats." I knew that was my only salvation to keep me from getting punished. But getting punished for what? Just being stupid? Yeah, probably so. Just being stupid would probably render down the wrath of my father. Certainly I would be the laughing stalk of all the kids at school, but I had my plan. The plan was all about the Red Rats. It was all the fault of the Red Rats.

Now all I had to do was to convince Mom and Dad that it was one of those Red Rats that I had lit off, one of those evil devils had taken off and immediately made a U turn and before I could duck, Whoosh…right over my head. I thought I had contrived a pretty good story and I would indeed stick to it. I decided to put my plan into action.

After lighting Red Rats for a while, I let out a big scream and ran to the house to tell them what happened. With a surprised look on their faces, I told Mom and Dad my story of how my hair got burned off. If they suspected the once magnificent Big Bertha, which was now back in the trash barrel with the top burned out and no insides left and looking much singed, they never said anything to me. They just shook their heads and agreed that those Red Rats were dastardly and what a lucky boy I was that it didn't put one of my eyes out.

Green Means GO!

My brother Yendor is always late. If you want to have him at your house at 6:00 p. m., you really need to tell him he must be there by 4:00. I had forgotten that fact when my brother Yendor and his wife Lena, our friends Tuna and his girlfriend Merry Moo, my wife Moodoo and myself had tickets for a kick-ass concert sixty miles away in the big city of Omaha.

We had tickets to see Cheap Trick, REO Speedwagon, Foghat, and Iron Butterfly. And we all loved live music, in fact Yendor and I were in a rock band together, so this concert seemed like a dream come true. Four great acts, are you kidding? Wow, what fun! One little problem though, this concert was in Omaha, sixty miles away and we were in the middle of a hard, cold winter. No matter, come hell or high water or in this case ice, a lot of ice, we were still going to go.

We were all set with our fantastic tickets in hand, and Lena had made arrangements for hotel rooms for all of us, since she worked at a large hotel chain and could get our rooms for almost nothing.

The concert was to start at 7:00 p. m. and I told Yendor to be at our house by 5:00, just to be safe. Did I mention that Yendor is always late? Tuna and Merry Moo were at our house waiting with us, watching the clock move to 5:00, then 5:30, then 5:45, then 6:00. This was, of course, before cell phones, so we just had to wait. Finally, at 6:15, Yendor and Lena arrived.

"Where the devil have you been?" I exploded. "We will never make it in time!"

"Relax, bro," Yendor said, "We have plenty of time."

I immediately thought we might be in real trouble as it appeared by this comment that Yendor had already been drinking heavily. "It is a little slick though," Yendor mused as he slid his feet on the heavy coating of ice in our driveway.

"A little slick," I said, noticing that the ice had a coating of water on top, and it was misting a heavy, freezing drizzle as well. To top it all off, Yendor's tires on the old green Chevy van, old Greenie, had less tread than a billiard ball. Perhaps Ron Popiel's spray-on hair would have helped these poor old tires. At this point, Moodoo came to the door and said that the concert was off. The state patrol had just closed the interstate to Omaha.

"Nonsense," said Yendor, "everybody get in the van!"

We all clambered into the old relic, but when Yendor tried to leave the parking lot, he just slid.

"That's it!" I said, "We will never even get out of here."

Yendor just laughed, lit a cigarette, and told us to push him to the street.

So, we did just that. We climbed back in and headed for the concert. We went to the interstate, and Yendor simply went around the barricades, and off we went.

"We won't make it in time." We all agreed. But Yendor just put the pedal to the metal and, with no tire tread and a lot of ice, we soon reached warp speed. Tuna said this was going to get us all killed. He and Merry Moo soon laid on the floor, either to avoid the impact of the impending crash, or maybe to get a little feeling-up time before we got to our destination.

Yendor, cool as a cucumber, got us to Omaha, into the parking lot, and into the building with time to spare. "Hang on," he shouted as we jumped out of the old Chevy.

Since Tuna, Merry Moo, Moodoo and I are all blind, Yendor and Lena decided to make a chain with all of us, and away we ran to the auditorium. Poor Merry Moo, she was at the end of the chain and was like the tail of a whip, which got cracked every turn we took. Yendor and Lena got us all to our seats and brought us large cups of beer, sitting down just as the first note blasted over the loudspeakers.

"I don't know how you did it, but you did it!" I said to Yendor over the loud rock music. He just smiled, took a sip from his beer, and lit up another cigarette.

The concert was indeed a blast, one of the best we ever heard. Afterwards, half drunk and nearly deaf, we spent the night in our hotel rooms and drank a few more beers before turning in for the night. The next morning, we drug ourselves out of bed and went for breakfast at Village Inn.

This is where Yendor and Lena nearly got into a huge fight, much to the amusement of the rest of us. It happened after we had finished breakfast, when the waiter asked Lena if she wanted the large brownie sundae that she was drooling over in the menu. Lena could not make up her mind about that huge sundae.

"Should I, or shouldn't I?" she asked.

Yendor, trying to be helpful but screwing up his words, said, "Go ahead, Lena, have the sundae, you ain't none too skinny anyway."

We all know what he meant, but it didn't come out that way. We all began to laugh at this comment.

"What?!" exploded Lena.

Yendor, now slightly panicked, tried again. "I mean, um, you are plenty heavy, honey!"

At this, the rest of us began laughing almost hysterically. This did not help. For the rest of the morning Yendor kept apologizing to Lena, but she kept very quiet. Of course, our incessant laughing probably didn't help poor Yendor either.

All in all, it was a fun adventure, Yendor and Lena are still together, despite the brownie sundae, but their old Chevy van Greenie has long since been turned into a horse trailer, probably with the same old bald tires.

Snorting Coke

Darlene Ronker was a big girl, just a year ahead of me in school in our small town of Pallywonkersville. Darlene, it seemed, always had a crush on me, and I do mean that literally, as it turned out one summer afternoon. Darlene and I were friends, though not really very close friends.

She did, on one occasion, while we were in junior high school, teach Boner Bently, my cousin Alabama, and me about the female anatomy of which we were then and forever more fascinated by the differences she showed us between boys and girls.

Darlene also knocked the snot out of me with a baseball bat, accidentally as it turned out. She was making a practice swing during our daily lunch-hour game of softball.

When she made a mighty swing, not just a 360-degree spin but more like a 720-degree spin, and managed to hit me right in the mid-section as I walked by. Purely an accident, but if she had known what would occur some years later, I think she might have beaten me severely and repeatedly with that same ball bat.

The day in question was in late May. Darlene was a senior in high school and I was a junior. We were both out for track and had gone to a track meet in Vertigo, a small town about 150 miles from Pallywonkersville. The trip mostly had to be traveled by dirt road, and it was an uncommonly hot day for May. The temperature about 95 degrees, and the track meet was a long one, not finishing until well after 7:00 p.m.

We were, of course, traveling in an old Blue Bird yellow school bus which had no bathroom and no air conditioning. It was an incredibly unbearable ride due to the heat, dust from the dirt road, and the awful roughness of the road. The bus danced like a drunk with the blind staggers. I do not know if the track meet was successful or not; I was hot and tired and more than a little miffed. The cans of Coke that I had brought along had been left in the sun and were so hot they were undrinkable. I feared they might explode at any moment. Oh, if I had only known.

As we traveled home, Darlene took up a seat at the back of the bus, being a senior, and I was in the seat directly in front of her. As I said, she had a crush on me and took this opportunity to show it by flirting. She pulled my hair and tweaked my ears. Then she laughed and snorted. Oh, god, how awful. I did not appreciate this treatment, but most of the rest of the track team were getting a huge charge out of my misfortune.

She pulled my hair, tweaked my ears, and laughed, and snorted. This was repeated over and over until I began to think more of revenge than of just getting her to stop.

Even though I had asked her to stop, because of the great fun she was having and because the others were egging her on, this continued for some time. What a miserable ride. As I said, I began to think of how I could get even once she stopped, but had not yet formulated my diabolical scheme.

Finally the obnoxious Darlene gave up and went to sleep. To say she was asleep would conjure up ideas of peaceful slumber, but this was not the case. Darlene snored like a small rhino, with her intake nearly sucking the air out of the bus for the rest of us. On her loud exhale, one might think the bus was under attack by either a hailstorm or a jet, buzzing quite low. This girl could snore, her mouth open with a stream of drool pooling on her shirt.

My cousin Chauncy was right. I did have a warped sense of humor, because I began to form a plan of both revenge and of what I thought might be pretty darn funny to everybody on the bus, even though many were asleep. My remaining can of Coke, as I said, was hot. Very, very hot. I began to wonder if I put the can right by her nose and pulled the pop top off, just how much would go up her nose. How large was her sinus cavity anyway? Well, a hot Coke might not be enough, it surely would need to be shaken up just a bit, right? I must have shaken the can of Coke for a full 5 minutes. Not even the paint shaker at the local hardware store could have done a better job than I had.

I turned around, positioned the can of Coke right between Darlene's nostrils, took hold of the pull tab, the old kind that pulled completely off, then I let her rip. Kaboosh!!! I do believe that the entire contents of the Coke went straight up Darlene's nose.

Darlene exploded! Her eyes opened wide in surprise and horror. Her sinus had just been violated by some brown, burning, foaming, icky substance. She began to snort, cough, wheeze, and bellow like an enraged bull elephant.

"Argh!" she screamed as Coke foam came frothing out of her nose and mouth. "Argh, argh," she bellowed, waking up the entire bus. "What the hell?" she sputtered, still trying to figure out just what had happened, her nose and sinus on fire. She looked like a rabid hippo with the burning red eyes, her mouth and nose foaming with the sticky, frothy brown liquid. What a sight!

Other kids were waking up to see this spectacle and they were beginning to laugh at Darlene, and this was making her more irate than hurt. "Argh," she was still foaming and burning.

I, of course, could not contain my laughter, even though I knew that soon she would figure out that I had exacted my revenge on her. Darlene gave me a look that said, you bastard, now you are gonna die! Still snorting Coke foam and choking Darlene looked at me. "I am gonna kill you !" she screamed.

The rest of the bus was nearly hysterical at this point, except for the bus driver, a middle-aged lady with a high-pitched voice that sounded like the Bee Gee's falsetto singing.

"Children, stop right now," she said.

By this time Darlene was clawing her way over the seat to get to me. I jumped to the next seat over, but Darlene roared and charged after me. As big as she was, she made the bus jump each time she jumped from seat to seat, which made everybody laugh all the more.

"Stop, please stop," pleaded the driver.

"You are dead meat, David!" Darlene hollered.

Even though I was faster than Darlene, what happened was inevitable. She caught me in the back of the bus and began to jump up and down on top of me.

"You bastard!" she snorted as she bounced up and down on top of me. I think she might have derived some sadistic sexual pleasure from all her bouncing and pouncing, I don't know. I covered my head and my package, just in case she decided to kick me there, and I laughed.

Even though it was pretty painful, Darlene got a standing ovation by the rest of the kids on the bus when she had finished, as they had never seen anything like this before, and they appreciated the show. My friends, Doogie and Boner, told me it was the funniest thing they had ever seen. Chauncy was right, I did have a warped sense of humor. I suppose he knew it would get me in trouble, but what the hell, it was worth the beating.

Goose-necked

My friend Doogie Blower is my age, and he has no children. I think I might know why that is the case. For one thing, he had an altercation with an electric fence at my farm when he was young, but he also had one other event happen that might have left his manhood null and void.

Doogie had a paper route in our small town, and I often helped with his route, mostly for lack of anything better for me to do. The papers would come in from the main hub, the paper lady would drop them off at one of Doogie's neighbors' yards and we would take it from there, separating the papers and putting them in Doogie's newspaper bag and away we would go.

This particular day we were waiting for the paper lady. It was a warm summer afternoon, and we were kicking back, waiting. I was propped up against a large elm tree, but Doogie was lying on his back, his legs spread slightly, his hands behind his head, his ball cap over his eyes and a sprig of grass in his mouth. What a nice, lazy afternoon. We were discussing baseball because we were both on the team, and we had a game that night. Doogie played both second base and pitcher, and I was both a pitcher and first baseman.

Everything was nice and calm, until my cousin Alabama rode up on his stingray bike. This appeared to be no big deal. Alabama simply rode his bike between Doogie's legs and stopped there. He joined in the conversation, and we waited for the papers. Alabama began to lift the front tire of his bike up in the air and drop it down, making it bounce between Doogie's legs. Did I detect some trouble ahead? I thought that it was a dangerous thing to do, right between Doogie's legs and all, but surely nothing bad would come of this, would it?

Alabama looked at me with a sinister grin, mouthed the words "Watch this," and backed his bike up about twenty yards and suddenly peddled like mad at Doogie. Not only did he pedal towards Doogie, he also popped a wheelie. Oh no, I thought, it could not happen, could it? Alabama had a big head of steam while Doogie, oblivious to the situation, just kept talking.

Alabama stomped on the brakes, apparently hoping to stop between Doogie's legs and give him a start. He overshot the target by a few inches. His front tire slammed down, not just between Doogie's legs, but directly on his gonads.

At this incredible pain, Doogie screamed, and suddenly sat up. Bad idea. His sudden forward thrust caused his forehead to make contact with the metal gooseneck of Alabama's bike. The sudden trauma caused him to fall backward, now with serious injury to both his head and lower region. Wow! Alabama and I looked at each other in awe, both realizing that this was a bad, bad thing. At this point, Alabama did the only thing he could. He quickly rode off into the sunset, as the paper lady arrived.

She asked me why Doogie was rolling around on the ground with one hand on his package and the other on his forehead and growling like a bear. I told her the only thing that came to mind, that he suffered from these rare seizures and that his mom told us all to leave him alone until he came out of them. This was good enough for her; she dropped off the papers and drove off.

Doogie's house was just a few houses away, so I ran and got his mom. I explained what happened, and she came to take care of Doogie. Since I appeared to be an accomplice in this event, I got the job of delivering Doogie's papers for about a month while he recovered. Alabama simply disappeared during this time, leaving it all up to me.

Doogie did have an incredibly-large goose egg, or was it a gooseneck egg for quite a long time. I don't know what his nether region looked like, I never asked to see it and he never offered to show it to me, although he did walk bow' legged for quite a while. Doogie still has no children to this day. Could this be the reason?

'Taint Funny

Sometimes when you are young, ignorance is bliss. Other times it is incredibly funny. This was the case one early spring day, when I was a lad of about eight years old. My dad Doonie and I were in the basement of our farmhouse. Dad was working on our lawnmower, getting it tuned up and ready for the coming summer grass and weed cutting. I was downstairs with him, not really helping, but rather looking at all of the fun things in our basement, full of junk and assorted other stuff.

Dad was facing away from me, bent over the mower with his legs slightly spread apart. This is a very important fact. Never ever leave your child alone with a lot of junk while your back is turned! I knew most of the stuff in the basement and nothing really seemed too exciting to me, until I spotted something new. I saw a long metal tube, about a foot-and -a -half long, nearly as big around as my arm, silver in color with a rubber handle on one end and two small prongs on the other end. What was this funny metal tube? I picked it up and examined it closely. I found that when I pushed in on the rubber handle, the tube made a buzzing sound, and a little blue spark went across the metal prongs. How neat.

As I surveyed this tube, it occurred to me that this little blue spark would probably tickle. Tickle my rear! Tickle my dad's rear is what I decided to try. Did I mention that the tube held eight large D cell batteries, and they were brand new? I looked at my dad Doonie. He was completely engrossed in the mower. This tickle was going to be easy, I thought.

I crept up behind him, aimed the prongs between his legs and pushed them against the "Taint" If you are not familiar with the word Taint, it taint the rectum and it taint the scrotum, it is right in between. Dad felt this, and just started to say, "What the devil," when I pushed in on the rubber handle. I do not know how much voltage the cattle prod contained, but it seemed to be quite a lot. As the electricity connected with Dad's nether region, he let out a blood-curdling scream and jumped straight up in the air.

This was an error, as our basement was not very deep and he slammed the top of his head into one of the rafters in the ceiling. Now he had two major pains, or was that three, including me? He began doing this hilarious dance, with one hand on top of his head and one hand on his now electrocuted crotch. He screamed cries of pain as well as obscenities. Wow, I don't think I ever saw anything as entertaining! Dad was dancing around, hollering and cursing, all at the same time. It suddenly occurred to me that I had better get out of the basement while I still had a chance, because once Dad figured out what happened, he would be mad as a wet hen, or a castrated bull.

I ran up the stairs, out of the house, and out to one of my favorite hiding places down in a canyon behind our house. This hiding place had come in handy on several other occasions. Pretty soon, Dad came outside, and I heard him say, "David, come here, I have something I want to show you." He said this several times, but I was pretty sure I knew what he wanted to show me, and I already knew what it was by this time and figured I did not need to see it again. Especially since I guessed he would feel turnabout, or around, was fair play.

Dad finally went to town for his morning coffee. Eventually I went back to the house, and Mom was still laughing. She even had tears in her eyes. I don't think Dad told his cronies at the bar what happened for fear of more ridicule, or of them adding insult to injury, but he had calmed down quite a bit by the time he got home. I am not sure what ever happened to the cattle prod. It was probably put away in a safe place, far, far away from any curious children.

Good Ol' Honest Abe

I recently went on a business trip to a conference in a large Midwestern metropolitan city with my friend Hoady and a couple business acquaintances, Delbert and good old Harry Terrace. It was your usual business conference, complete with meetings, breakfasts and luncheons, also long afternoon sessions. It was hard not to take a nap after you ate.

We had been there a couple of days, when after the close of the afternoon session, the four of us discussed going out to dinner. Hoady and I wanted to stay in the hotel and go to the Italian restaurant, where we had eaten the night before, but Delbert and Harry wanted to go elsewhere. Hoady and I were overridden in the decision of where to eat, and we decided to have our meal outside of the hotel.

The four of us ventured to a nearby mall, which had quite a few food establishments. We wanted to eat at a quality place that boasted of grand culinary delicacies. Instead, we chose a restaurant that sounded wonderful to Delbert and Harry. They decided that we should go to a place that would offer more than just food. They wanted the entertainment of scantily clad young women with rather large boobs.

So we went to the restaurant known as "Honkers". The atmosphere was clean, upscale and rather modern. The girls were all between the ages of twenty-one and twenty-five. They were very good looking and well-endowed, most of them would make a milk cow ashamed of their small hooters by comparison. Oh, they were so friendly in this Midwestern town.

We ordered our dinners, and they were very nondescript. Even though the food was bland, each time the waitresses came around, they made you feel special. They smiled and asked if we needed anything and coyly jiggled and bounced their boobs up and down, making us forget about the food. I suppose the food was adequate, but definitely nothing to brag about.

I was dunking my fries into some ranch dressing, when I noticed Delbert, his head bobbing from side to side and up and down, watching the girls bounce as they walked by our table. He looked like one of those dogs that so many people used to put in the back windows of their cars.

I also noticed that Delbert was drooling a bit like a man just ready to dive into a thick, juicy steak, but I knew a steak was not what he wanted to dive into and he could not control himself. You could take the boy out of the small town, but you could not take the small town out of the boy.

Hoady and Harry were discussing some matters, when Hoady made, what would seem to most observers, like a fairly innocent statement. Although I can't remember their entire earlier conversation, he and Harry were now working on splitting up our bill.

Being visually impaired, Hoady had given Harry a twenty-dollar bill, and Harry had given him back some change. Harry had simply said, "I think I gave you back the right amount."

"Don't worry about it, Harry," Hoady said, "I trust you as much as good old honest Abe Lincoln." That was when the feathers hit the fan!

Harry sat straight up in his chair and said "Abe Lincoln …why that no good rotten egg-sucking scum licking son of a dog's ass!"

Hoady and I were shocked by such an unexpected outburst by Harry. Hoady replied, "What do you mean, Harry? Abe Lincoln was a great president. He guided us through one of the darkest times in our history."

Harry responded with "Abe Lincoln …that no-good, worthless, blasphemous, sorry S. O. B!"

I, of course, began to find this conversation somewhat humorous. Delbert didn't seem to notice anything was going on, because his head was still bobbing up and down like some kind of mechanical dog.

Hoady again said, "Abe Lincoln was one of the best presidents that the United States has ever had. He freed the slaves!"

Harry responded, now standing up, his face all flushed and red," Why, that bastard Abe Lincoln …they should have killed him long before he was assassinated …that mother raper!"

At this point, the other people in the restaurant were starting to look at our table, and those very friendly waitresses from earlier, seemed to be giving us a lot of room, as they walked by very quickly. I would have liked something else to drink, but no waitresses wanted to get close to our table! Delbert didn't mind…his head still bobbed up and down.

Hoady would say, "Now calm down, calm down…"

Then Harry would respond, "Calm down?…well, that black-hearted son of a gun! He was the crookedest man in the history of the United States. They should have gotten rid of him years before!"

At this point, Hoady was starting to see that he had opened up a large can of worms and was trying to put the lid back on it. I could only wonder at what Abe Lincoln had done to Harry Terrance's family. Perhaps all of the women in his family as well as some of the menfolk had been buggered in the rear by a steady parade of Union soldiers during the Civil War. The Terrace family slaves, now free, watched the festivities, and may have broken into dance and song, chanting "Lincoln, Lincoln, Lincoln" while the Terrace family was being disgraced and defiled.

"Whoa whoa whoa…let's just calm down now," exclaimed Hoady.

"Who can calm down…when you're talking about a worthless no good murderous piece of dog vomit!" protested Harry.

The scene was continuing to escalate, and I was beginning to see that no one was going to get us out of this mess, but me. The idea of telling jokes popped into my head. Of course, nothing I came up with was a good one. The first one I thought of had to do with a nun, a priest, and a rooster. I don't think anyone laughed, in fact, they thought it was the most vulgar joke they had ever heard. At least, it got us off of the subject of Abe Lincoln, or so I thought.

Soon the waitress took our money and left quickly, trying to avoid this group of nuts as much as she could. She came back with our change, and the top bill, looking right at Harry, was a five-dollar bill with good old honest Abe staring right at him, and he exploded again.

"That worthless. no-good bastard!" Harry screamed. "I have to look at that god awful pig's butt everywhere I go!" He exploded. Before we knew it, we were being escorted out of Honkers and shoved out into the street, where a crowd had gathered to see what the yelling was all about. We dusted ourselves off and went back to the hotel and tried to keep a low profile during the rest of our trip.

From time to time, Hoady and I still speak of the trip we took with Delbert and Harry and what could have possibly set off our good friend Harry to rant and rave about our assassinated president, honest Abe Lincoln. Whatever it was, we decided never again to mention old honest Abe around him. I always thought it would be ironic, if at some point in time, Harry would be given the Abe Lincoln award for honesty. What a truly awesome response he would give for his acceptance speech, "I am here to accept this award for the Abraham Lincoln, the what? Abe Lincoln, Why that no good, rotten, yellow-bellied, scum-sucking, dirty son of a …"

Busted

Teevey was a great practical joker, and he certainly had a wonderful zest for life. Although Teevey had suffered through a plethora of medical problems, all caused by diabetes, he never gave in to the temptation to feel sorry for himself or for anybody else in his situation. He believed that if you can do anything at all in life, just do it!

Teevey had a large, two-story house that he had been remodeling himself, mostly after going blind and losing a leg to diabetes. He rented out the upstairs to a mutual friend, but the main floor of his house was, in those days, party central on most weekends. The parties generally consisted of my wife Donna, who was my girlfriend at the time, our friend Merry Moo, and a host of others that sometimes grew into crowds of thirty or forty.

No invitation was ever needed, just a hello to Teevey and you were in like Flint. Teevey always gave both Donna and Merry Moo a bad time, and they generally gave him back in spades what he could dish out, which pleased him to no end. He loved the challenge of both these wild women. It was in this tit for tat that Donna and Merry Moo came up with a truly diabolical plan to get Teevey, once and for all, with a joke he would be proud of them for hatching, but also one that Teevey himself probably could never match. Even I thought that the girls might have gone too far with this idea, but, what the hell, as long as it was not done to me, if you know what I mean. It would certainly be a gas if they could pull it off.

The four of us frequented a local eating establishment, Della's Diner, and this was where the plan would come together. Della, the owner of the restaurant, loved Teevey and did what she could to take care of him like a surrogate mother, because she felt that he needed some motherly advice from time to time. We did not know how Della would respond to this joke, since she was so protective of Teevey. The girls did not think they could risk letting her in on the proceeding for fear that she would let the cat out of the bag.

Donna and Merry Moo had invited Teevey to have lunch with us, and they could not wait for the fun. Donna, Merry Moo, and I arrived at Della's early to get a good table. We had a cup of coffee and waited for Teevey to arrive. Soon, in walked Teevey.

Della gave him a friendly "Hi, Teevey, my buddy, your friends are waiting for you." Friends, indeed. If they only knew what was coming, and soon, of course, they would. We soon engaged in conversation and laughter,

179

ordered our lunch, and ate it. When we were drinking our coffee, the joke arrived in the form of a police officer.

He said that he had an arrest warrant for Teevey. Teevey was dumbfounded. Della was having a conniption fit about what was going on, and Donna and Merry Moo were about to fall out of their chairs, laughing. The fact was that the police officer was simply there for a local charity that was doing a classic "Jail and Bail." You are turned in for a bogus crime, then you have to go to the police station and call all of your friends and family to donate money to spring you out. The officer had done his job so well that it had not appeared to be a fundraiser. It seemed that Teevey was truly being arrested for a crime.

Teevey began to protest, "But, officer, what did I do?"

The officer quickly responded, "You are charged with getting too frisky with little girls."

This got Donna and Merry Moo laughing so hard they could hardly breathe. Merry Moo said, "Tee hee, it sounds like you got the right man, officer!"

Teevey was incredulous, saying to Merry Moo, "This is not funny, I could be going to jail!"

Donna piped up, "Well, it is about time they start getting the perverts off the street."

Della was just about hysterical screaming, "What are you doing to my Teevey, you let my Teevey alone!"

I was laughing so hard that tears streamed down my face. "Don't just sit there, Dave," Teevey said, "help me out for god's sake!"

"Sorry," I said, "you are on your own. I don't want any trouble with the officer."

The whole scene was getting to be quite a spectacle, with the other patrons now watching intently, many of them older people, who were now siding with the officer to take the child molester downtown and give him what-for. I even remember a few comments about rubber hoses and the like being used on him.

Della kept saying that there had to be some kind of mistake. Teevey himself was getting pretty nervous and Merry Moo, Donna and myself were nearly rolling on the floor with laughter.

Finally, the officer said to Teevey, "Have you ever heard of Jail and Bail?" Teevey looked at him for a few seconds, and then it hit him what was going on.

"Who turned me in for this Jail and Bail?" Teevey was fuming now.

The officer responded, "This girl right there," pointing to Merry Moo.

"Why, those rotten little wenches," Teevey said, seeing that he was the butt of a successful prank. "Well," Teevey started, "I can't go downtown with you officer, you see I am a diabetic, and I just ordered lunch. I have to eat. Being a diabetic, I have to have my food at regular times."

The officer was about to say he understood, when Merry Moo pulled out the trump card. From her purse she produced a sack lunch for Teevey, complete with sandwich, potato chips, an apple, a pop, and even a napkin. "Tee hee," Merry Moo said, "Here's your lunch, Teevey, no need for you to stay here!"

"Well," the officer said, "it looks like you can go with me after all."

Della was nearly hysterical, "Please don't take my Teevey away, please," she kept saying, not realizing yet that this was a joke. She just wanted to keep her friend from being arrested.

I don't know if she ever truly forgave Donna and Merry Moo for this prank, but Teevey never forgot it, vowing every time I spoke with him that he was going to get even. He just needed to find a prank that could top theirs, but he never did, although he did try.

All Rolled Up...

My dad Doonie had bad luck with vehicles. Not all of them, just a few, such as his prized 1965 Chevy Impala, which burned up one day at the bottom of the big hill. A few days later, Dad received his letter that the car had a defect and could burn up when the engine mount broke. The engine could rise up, breaking the fuel line, and spraying gasoline on the motor, causing a fire. Yep, exactly what happened!

My Dad would not, of course, ever think about a lawsuit. That was not his style. Nope, he just lost a car and took it in the shorts. So, here we were on a nice summer afternoon, Dad was out on the family hog farm, using his prized Ford pickup to do farm work. This was a nice truck, a Ford F 250, blue and white with a big motor, and probably the best feature to Doonie, it ran like a striped assed ape. Did I mention that it was an automatic, with the gearshift on the column? Yep, the old three on the tree.

Well, Dad had purchased several steel panels for the hog lot earlier that day, and they were in the back of the truck. These panels were made of heavy gauge steel wire, about as big around as a ball point pen and making approximately four-inch squares. The panels were twelve feet long and four feet wide, so they stuck out of the back of the truck a ways. Since nobody was around to help Dad, he decided to unload the panels by himself. Bad idea, really bad idea, and Dad should have known, with his previous track record, not to attempt such things by himself. Oh, well, he never listened to any of us anyway.

So, he backed the truck up to the hog lot fence, and rather than shutting the truck off, he left it running, in park. Another bad idea. Dad then proceeded to the back of the truck and pulled on the first panel to drag it out of the truck bed. Apparently, the jostling of the truck caused old blue to fall into gear, yep, reverse. As the old truck roared backwards, Dad, rather than jumping out of the way, ducked instead. One more bad idea! The hog panel, now hanging down to the ground, caught on something. With Dad ducking down, it began to roll him up like a burrito. As Dad screamed and covered his head with his hands, he was rolled up and drug under the truck.

Luck was with him a little bit, because the door of the truck caught on a fence post and stopped the progress of the truck, leaving Dad rolled up, horizontal, with his hands over his face and his head by one rear tire and his feet by the other. The pickup continued to run, with the exhaust belching directly in Dad's face. All rolled up with no place to go!

It's hard to say how long Dad was rolled up. I am sure it seemed like an eternity to him. But eventually, my brother Yendor came home from wherever he had been. He began to wonder where Dad was, and why his pickup was running in the hog lot. Yendor said that, as he got closer to the truck, he heard a muffled, "Help me, please help me!" Yendor looked around, but saw nobody. Again he heard the muffled, "Help, oh, please help me!" Not seeing anybody, Yendor decided to shut the pickup off, that is when he finally saw Dad.

"What the dang is going on?" Yendor looked under the truck, and yep, Dad seemed to be alive, but Yendor couldn't tell how badly he was hurt.

"Help me quick," Dad pleaded.

Yendor looked over the situation and decided the only way to help Dad was to drive the truck forward, getting it away from the wire-rolled Doonie.

After he accomplished the task, Yendor went to the back to see what he needed to do next. What a picture, Dad rolled up like an egg roll and completely unable to move.

"Get me out of this mess!" Dad demanded.

Yendor soon realized Dad was okay, only his pride was dented a bit.

"Sure, Dad, I will get you out of this mess." But first he asked, "Well, I was wonderin' if I could borrow the car tonight for my big date, and, well I could sure use fifty bucks for, you know…"

"Hell, no!" Dad bellowed, as best as he could with his hands over his face.

"Okay," said Yendor coolly. "I guess I will get you out of there, but I am kinda' hungry, I think I might have to go to town and get me something to eat. I don't think I have enough strength to get you out of there right now…"

"Goldurn it, get me out of here!" Dad sputtered again.

"Well," said Yendor, "I might muster up enough strength if I could borrow the car…"

"Oh, all right," muttered a defeated Doonie, "just hurry up!"

"Sure thing," said Yendor. "I think I will need seventy five bucks though, this is gonna' make me mighty hungry."

"Little monster," muttered Dad.

Yendor had to go to the neighbors, the McKlonskys, to borrow bolt cutters, and they had to help him. Mostly to see the predicament Doonie had gotten himself into, and to get a good laugh at Doonie's expense as well. Oh yes, a few days later, Dad got a letter from Ford in the mail warning him that his Ford truck had a defect, and you guessed it. The truck could fall into reverse if the motor was left running. Dad had a minor explosion and lit his cigarette with the flaming letter.

Electrification

Doogie Blower and I were the best of friends from the age of ten until we went through high school, which is when we started going our separate ways. Our hometown of Pallywonkersville was where we both grew up, and people said that we were nearly inseparable, like twin boys from separate mothers. Doogie, his brother Gunner, and their parents, moved into the house next door to my grandparents, Nanna and Gaga.

This happened the summer that Doogie and I turned ten. Doogie and I became friends and did everything together since they lived so close to my grandparents. Doogie was fascinated with my life, since I lived on a farm. I was intrigued with him as well, because he was a city kid. We spent many hours together, playing baseball, riding our bikes, swimming at the town pool, learning about the naked female anatomy from his Dad's *Playboy* magazines, and discussing our city and country lives.

It was a treat for me to go into town during our summer vacation to play with Doogie, as well as Doogie to come to our farm. Doogie and I learned a lot over the next few years, such as chewing tobacco from the tobacco plug that my grandfather had given me, complete with a small, sharp knife to cut it with. We mistakenly tried out our tobacco during a baseball game one hot July day and both got rather green around the gills after swallowing some of the foul stuff.

I found that there was a lot that Doogie needed to learn about the farm. For example, you should not try to rope or ride a pig, eggs do fall from the butt of a chicken, barbed wire fence is for keeping the mean hogs in their pens, and I am sure there were a multitude of other things he needed to learn.

The hardest lesson that Doogie learned one summer was due to my prodding. For some reason, I was mad at Doogie and had been plotting a way to get back at him. The fact that I don't remember what he had done, and the severity of my retaliation, shows that he probably still owes me a good one.

Doogie's Mom had dropped him off at our house on this particular day for the afternoon and would pick him up later. We made our usual rounds on the farm, up in the tree house, down in the canyon with our pellet guns, and had eventually made it back to the house. It was at this time that I put my evil plan into motion.

"Doogie," I said casually, "Have you ever seen an electric fence?"

Doogie pondered the question and then told me that he had not seen one before, and furthermore, what was an electric fence and what was it used for? I told him that it is a single wire fence that is hooked up to electricity and keeps animals penned. "If an animal touches it, they will get a big charge of electricity."

I could tell that Doogie was skeptical of what I was telling him. "You mean that this little wire can keep hogs in better than a barbed wire fence?" Doogie asked.

"Yep, it keeps them in real good. It shocks them real bad, and they shake and will never try to get out again." I tried to be real cool with my answers, so Doogie wouldn't get wise. "This electric fence is real powerful and is plugged right into the electricity. It's not just run by some old car battery." Then I decided to try my hand at getting Doogie hooked. "The fact is that this particular fence is made by NASA. It is real special because it even repels water, so it won't short out if it rains or gets wet in any way."

Doogie was wide-eyed at this and got really curious. "You mean you got this from NASA, he asked?"

"We didn't just get it from NASA ourselves. They have been working on these sorts of newfangled inventions for a long time and are finally now letting folks know about them. Dad was very lucky because someone he knows almost got to be an astronaut, and he helped Dad get this special fence."

Doogie was incredulous, "You mean that it really repels water?"

"Yep, "I said. "It doesn't matter how much water there is or how little, you just can't get it close to the fence. It gets a couple of inches from it and just goes right around it."

"I don't believe it," Doogie said. "How can it do that?"

I tried hard to hook him. "I'm really not sure; only NASA knows. I can only tell you that it works like a charm. I even tried it myself."

Doogie just looked at me, and then his eyes narrowed, "What did you do to try it out?" he asked.

"Well," I said, "I tried to pee on that fence and you just can't do it," I told him emphatically. "I'll even show you, and I bet you a dollar that you can't hit the fence with your pee. I know that you just can't do it," I exclaimed. I unzipped my pants and started peeing towards the fence, making sure the yellow stream missed it.

"See" I said, "I can't even get close to it. I'll bet you a dollar that you can't do it either. I will even let you hold my dollar, just to be fair."

Doogie watched intently as my urine stream seemed to go toward the fence, then swerve around it. "Come on Doogie" I egged him on, "this is the easiest dollar you will ever get from me. This will prove to you that NASA made this fence, and it's really waterproof."

Doogie was finally hooked, I don't know if it was for the money or to prove me wrong, but for whatever reason, he decided to try it. He unzipped his pants, took out his water-weenie, and took careful aim, as if he would not have enough pee to properly test the fence. Then he let her rip, a beautiful, strong, yellow stream that headed straight for the fence.

I suppose I knew what I was doing here was seriously wrong, but I owed Doogie, and he was about to get his payback.

Doogie truly believed by now that the pee would not hit the fence and that would be the end of that. But the stream hit the electric fence. There was a bright blue spark which traveled back up the stream and connected with Doogie's wet Willie. The next reaction was even more than I had anticipated. Doogie shot backwards, let out a tremendous howl, and then hit the ground. He didn't just lie there, he rolled and writhed, he growled and made hilarious faces, he squirmed and peed all over himself, not seeming to be able to let go of himself either. He rolled, growled and writhed for several seconds.

I knew that perhaps I had gone too far, really too far, and that he might be seriously hurt. I must admit that, even though I was worried, the payback was complete. Doogie would have to think long and hard on how to top this one. My only dilemma now was to explain this event to my Mom, who was coming towards us from the house.

She decided to see what we were doing because Doogie's Mom would be coming soon to pick him up. I figured there would be no use in getting into a lot of trouble by telling the truth right here, and I knew Doogie wouldn't disagree with me.

"What on earth is going on? Mom asked. She saw Doogie rolling around and writhing in mud, made by his own urine.

"Mom, you know how city kids are, I tried to tell Doogie not to pee on the electric fence but he just wouldn't listen to me," I told her.

Doogie looked up and gave me the dirtiest look ever, as if to say "you bastard," but no words would come out. Only a sort of moaning and growling sound emerged from his lips, which struck me as even funnier. I began to laugh and that's when Mom scolded me, and said that I shouldn't enjoy other people's misfortunes, because he did not know any better. I was sure that Doogie would not be willing to tell his folks the truth that I got him, hook, line and sinker.

It would be better to just go with the line that he didn't know any better. It was a long time before Doogie came to our farm again, and I'm not sure if it was because he didn't want to, or if his parents were afraid to bring him out because of what had happened last time. To this day, Doogie still hasn't paid me back, knock on wood. Thank goodness, wood isn't an electric conductor.

"A" is for Alabama

Alabama is my cousin, and also a good friend. He obtained the name Alabama one night after ingesting much too much alcohol and perhaps other things. When we asked him his name, all he could say, in a slow and stupefied way, was, "Al uh bama." This seemed hilarious to us, since we had all had some alcohol as well. We then asked where he was from, and again the answer was, "Alabama." Every question we asked of him, the answer was the same, and as the saying goes, Alabama was born. This name is what Alabama goes by to this very day.

One New Year's Eve, Alabama and I went to our friend Murphy's house for a big party. This was to be a party to end all parties, and the multitude gathered there were all having a blast. They all thought they were having a blast, that is, until the wee hours of the morning, long after sane people had left, and all that remained were the passed-out drunks littering the house.

It appeared that the only two people left conscious were Murphy, being the good host that he was, and me. We were just shooting the proverbial breeze and surveying the littered landscape of drunks, commenting on what lightweights they all were. We were really surprised at Alabama, the great partier, who was passed out on the kitchen floor, having knocked over the 50-gallon trash can, so that he was lying half in the trash can and half on the kitchen floor with a large circle of empty cans and bottles surrounding him.

"What a lightweight Alabama is tonight," Murphy said. "I wonder what it would take to wake him up." Murphy kicked Alabama's foot, no response. Murphy then tossed half a glass of water, or beer, in Alabama's face. Still no response.

"I guess he is as totaled as everybody else, just as well give up." I said.

At this point, Murphy got a wicked smile and said "I know how to wake this joint up!" He went to the kitchen cupboard, opened the door and laughed. "I thought I might still have these!"

"What did you find?" I queried. Murphy turned around, still laughing, and showed me a large package, perhaps 1000, of Black Cat inch-and-a-half firecrackers left over from the Fourth of July.

"Dear god, no," I said.

"Dear god, yes." Murphy said, and he laughed a devilish laugh.

Murphy opened up the package and calmly lit a cigarette. He smiled and said, "Do you think Alabama can sleep through this?"

"You know this will make one hell of a mess." I said. "Some of the others might even crap themselves, and Alabama has been known to use my clothes hamper for a toilet as well."

Murphy laughed a wicked laugh again and looked at his cigarette and then at the Black Cats. "Here goes!" he said and lit the fuse.

I jumped back, and Murphy gave the Black Cats a toss. "Dear lord!" I gasped as the Black Cats landed across Alabama's chest. I don't think even Murphy thought that would happen, but it was too late now. As the thunder of 1,000 Black Cats hit the room, pandemonium ensued. One can only imagine what the crowd of passed-out new guests had immediately running through their heads.

As the thunder of what sounded like machine gun fire blasted away, people screamed and went into a panic. Some people flew out of their chairs, only to run into walls, furniture, or other panicked people. The screams were fantastic in their terror. Murphy and I burst into near hysterical laughter just witnessing this mad scene.

Oh yeah, what about Alabama? As the first of the Black Cats erupted on his chest, covered by a nylon disco shirt, Alabama sat upright, his eyes wide open with surprise, and then he uttered the words that made Murphy and me almost stop breathing with more laughter.

Alabama simply said, "Whoa, Dude!" And laid back down and went to sleep while the rest of the Black Cats exploded both on and around him. At the same time the other people were still screaming in terror, running around, and trying to make sense of the scene they found themselves in. When it was all over, the house was a complete wreck, with broken furniture, holes in walls, broken bottles, knocked-over cans, and of course, Alabama sleeping peacefully, half in and half out of the trash can in the kitchen. Most of his new disco shirt was burned and ruined, and burn marks covered his chest and stomach.

The smell of gunpowder was tremendous, even creating a sort of fog in the house. Murphy talked me into helping clean up the mess. For some unknown reason everybody else left after the rude awakening, muttering veiled threats and revenge.

Alabama woke up well after the house was cleaned up, and when he asked us what the hell happened to him, all we could say was "Alabama go Boom!" and laugh.

Dyne-o-mite

Well, here it was again, the Fourth of July. It was one of those holidays that usually held some bizarre twists or exciting turn of events for my family. This year I was at home alone, late in the middle of the afternoon. My mom and dad had gone off to Kansas to buy illegal fireworks with my little brother Yendor and sister Pretzel. Oh yes, the good old days when traditional family values really meant something. My grandma Nanna was going to come out and enjoy the festivities with us later that evening.

There I was, with nothing in particular to do, just a lazy hot Fourth of July. I was wondering what kinds of firecrackers Mom and Dad would bring back from Kansas. I was hoping for the big ones, such as Bottle Rockets, M-80's and Cherry Bombs... you know the ones that really go "Boom!" Pretty soon I noticed a car coming down the road. It looked quite familiar.

Low and behold, it was my older cousin, Chauncy Beerbomb. Chauncy was an interesting fellow, a practical joker, someone who liked to play with rattlesnakes and that sort. The kind of cousin that you love to see come to visit. He always had some tall tales to share with us, and mischievous things to do. Some years earlier, he and another cousin had nearly scared my dad to death by dressing up in a gorilla costume.

He rolled down our lane and pulled into the yard. He jumped out of the car and asked where my mom and dad were. I told him that they had gone off to Kansas to get fireworks for tonight.

Chauncy said, "Well, I have a little Fourth of July surprise for them, especially your dad. This sounded like a fun time because, as everyone in the county knows, my dad was a goosey-loosey. He was a spittin' image of Don Knotts, Fred Sanford, and George Jefferson all wrapped up into one. If someone yelled "snake" he would jump ten feet off the ground.

Chauncy told me that he thought that this was going to be a lot of fun! I asked, "What do you have?"

Chauncy grinned and exclaimed "just a little firecracker." He reached into the back seat of his car and pulled out not one, not two, but three sticks of dynamite. Yes, real dynamite. Chauncy worked at the sandpit and sometimes dynamite was used to either loosen some of the sediment down below to get better rock and gravel, or to bring some fish to the surface and have a good fish fry that night. Anyway, Chauncy had a license to light dynamite and here it was. I had never seen real dynamite before, but now I was staring right at it. Those big beautiful red sticks.

"Wow…what are we going to do with this?"

Chauncy said, "Well, we gotta find a good place for this little surprise."

"Dad hates that old John Deere combine," I said, "maybe we should just blow it up."

"No," said Chauncey, "He might get a little mad at us for that one."

We looked around the farm for a while, and all at once we saw it, the perfect place. In a field not too far from our house was a huge stump of a cottonwood tree. Dad and I had tried unsuccessfully, any number of ways to pull that old stump out of the field. We had tried with shovels, used crowbars, and even attached chains to the tractors to pull this massive stump out. My dad had finally given up, temporarily, of course. But there the stump stood, a monument of futility to my dad, just mocking him and giving me an education on curse words, many of which I had never heard before. At places, our shovels had dug around the huge tree's roots to no avail.

Chauncy said, "Here's our number-one candidate." Being an expert in dynamite, Chauncy knew just where to put it. He carefully placed the dynamite under the stump, and we went back to the house to indulge in a cold soda and perhaps, for Chauncy, it was a beer. Then Chauncy cut two fuses, both the same length.

I asked, "Why two fuses?"

He said, "So we know exactly when it will go off. We never want any surprises with dynamite. We are always in control." After he had cut the fuses, he lazily lit one, and we watched as he used the second hand on his wristwatch to decide just how long it was going to take for the explosion. I did likewise. Chauncy took the other fuse and precisely attached it to the dynamite.

By this time, it was late afternoon. We waited patiently for Mom and Dad to get home. Shortly they returned, and it was beginning to get the right time for fireworks, just about dusk. The little ones had to get to bed before too long, excited as they were for the fireworks. Nanna had arrived at the farm to watch the Fourth of July festivities. Everyone was delighted to see Chauncy there to help celebrate.

Dad said, "What are you doing out here, Chauncy?"

He calmly said, "Well, Doonie, I got a little Fourth of July surprise for ya'. Gotta a little Roman Candle out there behind the stump."

My dad wanted to go check out the firework. But Chauncy insisted that he sit down and we would all watch it together. Oh, what an event! I had run to the house to gather lawn chairs for everyone. There in the yard, not too far from the house, but also not too far from the stump, only about 50 yards away or so, the whole family sat waiting for this wonderful Roman candle that Chauncy promised would be a spectacular sight, something none of us had ever seen before and would never forget.

He went out to light the fuse and came back to join us. We all waited for the big event.

Dad hollered, "How long is this gonna take?" My dad was always the impatient one. I knew from my watch, it was going to be another thirty seconds or more.

"Any time now, Doonie, it takes these fuses a little while to light," exclaimed Chauncy.

My Dad got up to go and check out the big firecracker to make sure that it was still lit, but Chauncy said "NO, no, no…just wait right here, we'll give it another thirty seconds or so."

I knew that would be just perfect! I wanted to watch the stump, but I also wanted to see the reactions of everyone in my family. As it turned out, I ended up seeing both. The stump seemed to simply disappear in this incredible "Kaboom!!!"

To this date, some forty years later, I have never heard anything like it. To say it was a thunderous sound would be a vast understatement. The looks on my family's faces were priceless. They were looks of absolute surprise and sheer terror. Mouths wide open and eyes as big as dinner plates. Chauncy was already laughing by the time that it had gone off, and I was in awe.

To my amazement, with this mighty explosion came incredible amounts of dirt clods and pieces of stump, flying over our heads and showering us and the house, from the place where the once proud and mighty tree stump stood a moment ago.

The screams from Nanna, my Mom, brother, and sister were incredible. I don't know if my dad screamed, but he certainly let out a few whoops and hollers. Terror was the rule of the day. At this point, not knowing exactly what had happened, the fight or flight response had taken hold in everybody. It was a mad race to the house, as dirt fell down like light rain. Even though my Mom and Dad were in their prime, I thought they would be the first to get to the house, but that was wrong. My Nanna reached the house first. She was a little bit of a thing, five foot four and about 110 pounds. She was wearing a dress, high heels, and a hat, because she always dressed so stylishly.

Nanna led the pack, with one hand on her hat and the other on her skirt, as she ran the 50-yard dash to the house that would have been record setting. The rest of my family was not far behind, except for Chauncy and me.

We didn't move as we were laughing hysterically and rolling on the ground as we kept the vision of the explosion in our minds. Of course, when it was all said and done, after Mom, Dad and Nanna came to the conclusion that Chauncy and I had a hand in this explosion, and that God had not thrown down a mighty bolt of lightning and thunder for our sins, Chauncy was banished from our farm for quite a while. Any time when my mother or father saw him in town, they would give Chauncy the dirtiest look possible.

For my part in the dreaded conspiracy, there was an incredibly large hole to fill. This massive crater was big enough to hold a small car. Dad mentioned several times that it would certainly be large enough to bury both Chauncey and me and that nobody would ever miss us. It took me quite a while to fill that hole but with every shovelful I tossed in, I had to snicker in spite of myself, re-living the Moment of Terror that Chauncey brought to the farm that hot Fourth of July.

David Hunt

Riding Too Tall in the Saddle

Billy Ditto and I were, and still are, best of friends. We were thrown together back many moons ago when we both attended the School for the Blind. Billy is a true Native American, and we spent almost all of our free time shooting the breeze and drinking beer and smoking cigarettes. Both of us seemed to love to hear the tall stories the other would tell, and we both had many of them.

While I had only been blind for a short time due to diabetes, Billy had been blind all his life, so we did have a few differences in our perceptions of the world. As part of our training program, we frequently had outings to do what sighted folks thought were normal, but we thought were insane. On this occasion we were going to go to a ranch on the edge of town and go horseback riding. Some of the other students were scared to death by this event, but Billy and I thought this would be a hoot.

We thought that these horses were broken down old nags, and there would be no danger of them going too fast. Wrong answer, Dave. The truth was that this ranch trained horses to work cattle, and they were very fast and responsive. Billy and I both thought that we knew all about horses because had grown up on a farm, and Billy was a Native American. Oh, we sure made a mess when we tried to impress! Since we knew it all, we listened very little to the instructions given to us by the folks at the ranch.

We mounted our horses and started out to the pasture, slowly at first, then a little faster. "Let's make these old nags move!" I exclaimed.

"Giddyap, you old nag!" barked Billy. We kicked our horses in the sides, and to our amazement they took off like rocket horses from Hades. I was nearly in shock, not expecting such a response. I pulled back on the reins, and the horse stopped on a dime, nearly throwing me over his head. Billy's horse took off, back toward the barn. I began working with my horse a little more carefully, and found that he could turn a circle fast enough to spin me out of the saddle. I was impressed. This was not what I expected, and it was fun.

I rode for quite a while, enjoying the whole experience, and then I headed for the barn. When I got there, they were all laughing.

"What is going on?" I asked. Through the laughter somebody said it was too bad that I could not see Billy.

"Why is that?" I asked.

Well," one of our instructors said, "Big Chief Talks a Lot came roaring back to the barn, riding straight up in the saddle."

"So?" I answered.

"Well," they said, "the barn door was about seven feet tall, and Billy's head was about eight feet tall."

"Oh my," I said, starting to realize what had happened.

"Yep," said our instructor, "the horse ran straight in to the barn at warp speed and Billy, well his feet and body went through, but his face did not, and he was scraped right off the back of Old Rocket and landed on his duff with his teeth knocked loose!"

I went over to where Billy was sitting down and asked, "So what happened, partner?"

I think he tried to say, "Oh shut up!" but it did not come out quite right with his teeth loosened and his lips the size of a softball. I knew if I laughed any more he would probably kick me, so I just shook my head and said, "Yep, them fast horses are like fast women, get you in trouble every time."

Billy muttered "uh huh," and closed his eyes and then groaned.

I could not resist saying, "Yep, I wonder if any of those fast women would like a kiss with those big lips?" I am sure if looks could kill I would be dead, but Billy just muttered something incoherent and closed his eyes again. It took a lot of beer and cigarettes for Billy to get back to normal. I do not know if he ever lost any of his teeth, but he sure did have mighty big lips for a while. Billy never again spoke of going horseback riding, or the trip to the dude ranch with the broken down old nags. But, from time to time, one of the other students at the school for the blind would make a horse whinny sound when Billy walked down the hall.

More about the Author

David Hunt has found humor in many situations, and today, because of this, he is an excellent joke and storyteller. He has maintained this humorous look at life, even though he has experienced severe health problems, such as diabetes, kidney failure, blindness, and a kidney/pancreas transplant.

David met the love of his life, Donna, who is also blind, and together they both perceive and laugh at the humorous world around them.

His book, "Welcome to Pallywonkersville", is a hilarious look at his life as a youth in a small, rural community, and is sure to bring you much laughter as you read about his delightful, and often frightful, escapades.

David is a talented musician and has written several songs and recorded them on a CD, titled "Sunshine." These songs are about his wife Donna and also about the loss of some of their close friends over the years. His mother's struggle with Alzheimer's disease inspired him to write the song, "Beautiful Mind". David also has recorded some funny parodies, which can be viewed on YouTube.

He and his wife Donna currently live with their two cats in the Midwest and together will always look for the brighter sides of life.

Made in the USA
Las Vegas, NV
16 June 2023

73506131R00128